Warwickshire County Council

- 6 MAY 2015			
Lea 7/18.			
12|10|23		 D0727187	

This item is to be returned or renewed before the latest date above. It may be borrowed for a further period if not in demand. **To renew your books:**

- **Phone the 24/7 Renewal Line 01926 499273 or**
- **Visit www.warwickshire.gov.uk/libraries**

Discover ● Imagine ● Learn ● with libraries

Warwickshire
County Council

Working for
Warwickshire

ROBIN WILLIAMS

WHEN THE LAUGHTER STOPS
1951–2014

EMILY HERBERT

JOHN BLAKE

Published by John Blake Publishing Ltd,
3 Bramber Court, 2 Bramber Road,
London W14 9PB, England

www.johnblakepublishing.co.uk

www.facebook.com/johnblakebooks 📘
twitter.com/jbbooks 📧

This edition published in 2014

ISBN: 978 1 78418 300 4

British Library Cataloguing-in-Publication Data:

A catalogue record for this book is available from the British Library.

Design by www.envydesign.co.uk

Printed in Great Britain by CPI Group (UK) Ltd

1 3 5 7 9 10 8 6 4 2

Papers used by John Blake Publishing are natural, recyclable products made
from wood grown in sustainable forests. The manufacturing processes conform
to the environmental regulations of the country of origin.

Every attempt has been made to contact the relevant copyright-holders,
but some were unobtainable. We would be grateful if the
appropriate people could contact us.

'Carpe diem. Seize the day, boys.
Make your lives extraordinary.'

John Keating (Robin Williams), *Dead Poets Society* (1989)

CONTENTS

TRIBUTES

The following is a selection of the tributes paid to the late Robin Williams.

Bill Cosby @BillCosby: I'm stunned!

Melissa Joan Hart @MelissaJoanHart: Beyond upset about one of my idols passing away tragically!! RIP Robin Williams.

Lindsay Lohan @lindsaylohan: Mr. Williams visited me the first day of filming The Parent Trap. I will never forget his kindness. What an enormous loss. My condolences.

Joel McHale @joelmchale: RIP @robinwilliams. You were one of the very best that ever was. You were one of my heroes. #RobinWilliams

Anna Kendrick @AnnaKendrick47: O Captain! My Captain! Rise up and hear the bells. Rise up, for you the flag is flung, for you the bugle trills.

Kirstie Alley @kirstiealley: RIP sweetie... you made the world laugh for decades... Rest a while xxxooo

Jane Lynch @janemarielynch: Our loss. Orson's gain. #RIPRobinWilliams

Rita Wilson @RitaWilson: I am heartbroken. Dear, sweet friend, Robin Williams, gone. Our prayers for peace to all his friends and family, his beautiful children.

Chris Colfer @chriscolfer: Robin Williams was my hero growing up. You know someone is special when the whole world considers them family.

Jeremy Piven @jeremypiven: my father took me to see Robin Williams do an improv set. Never seen anything like it, he was a spirit like no other. Will never forget him.

John Stamos @JohnStamos: god no. The first autograph I ever got: Dear money, send mom. Robin Williams.

Lori Loughlin @LoriLoughlin: I'm shocked and saddened over the loss of Robin Williams. I had the great pleasure of working with him on Old Dogs. #RobinWilliams

Mindy Kaling @mindykaling: I am named after a character from a Robin Williams TV show when my parents still lived in Africa. He meant so much, to so many, so far away.

Lena Dunham @lenadunham: Just shared a moment of silence on the set for Robin Williams, a man who brought so much laughter, joy and healing to so many.

Kathy Griffin @kathygriffin: I met this sweet, generous & brilliant man Robin Williams in 1991. Here we are with HIS idol Jonathan Winters. #RIP.

TRIBUTES

Queen Latifah @IAMQUEENLATIFAH: Thanks for the years of feel good laughter. RIP Robin Williams.

Meredith Vieira @meredithvieira: I know he and his buddy Jonathan Winters are making the angels laugh out loud.

Ellen DeGeneres @TheEllenShow: I can't believe the news about Robin Williams. He gave so much to so many people. I'm heartbroken.

Scott Weinger @ScottWeinger: Farewell to my childhood hero and my Genie. The world won't be the same without him.

Debbie Allen @msdebbieallen: OMG I am so devastated. What a loss for the world #riprobinwilliams.

Mandy Moore @TheMandyMoore: Honored to have worked w such a bright light and brilliant man. Love and prayers to his family and friends. #RIPRobinWilliams.

John Mayer @JohnMayer: The first thing I ever wanted to be when I grew up was Robin Williams' inhabiting of Popeye. #RIPRobinWilliams. How awesome a contribution Robin Williams made to the world, that millions of people (and I) are now feeling real, deep human loss. So sad.

Goldie Hawn @goldiehawn: Oh Robin... Our hearts are broken. Rest in peace darling. We loved you.

Sesame Street @sesamestreet: We mourn the loss of our friend Robin Williams, who always made us laugh and smile.

Cher @cher: Oh Robin. He was Sweet LOVELY,Man.

He ran high voltage, Mind Always Going, It was who he was. I Know Well… Many X's from High There is Only Low. So Sad.

Jessica Chastain @jes_chastain: Robin Williams changed my life. He was a great actor and a generous person. Through a scholarship, he made it possible for me to graduate college. His generous spirit will forever inspire me to support others as he supported me. He will forever be missed.

CHAPTER ONE

A MUCH-LOVED MAN

'What I might do is watch Mrs. Doubtfire. *Or* Dead
Poets Society *or* Good Will Hunting *and I might be
nice to people, mindful today how fragile we all are, how
delicate we are, even when fizzing with divine madness
that seems like it will never expire.'*

RUSSELL BRAND, 'ROBIN WILLIAMS' DIVINE MADNESS
WILL NO LONGER DISRUPT THE SADNESS OF THE WORLD',
THE *GUARDIAN*, AUGUST 2014

11 August 2014 and the world was in profound shock.
Robin Williams, the Oscar-winning actor, comedian
and all-round comic genius, had been found dead at his
home in Tiburon, just outside San Francisco. He was only
sixty-three. What had happened – a heart attack, a stroke?
Recently he hadn't been seen much in public but no one

1

outside his immediate circle had been aware that anything could have been badly wrong.

Quite how wrong, however, soon became all too clear. For this wasn't a tragic medical emergency, rather it seemed that the talented but tormented comedian had taken his own life. The Marin County Sheriff's office put out a statement. '[It] suspects the death to be a suicide due to asphyxia,' it said. In other words, Williams had hanged himself. The world was aghast: Robin Williams was not just a popular actor but a much-loved one too. Generations had grown up watching his films; in his personal life he was known to be kind and generous too. Yes, he'd had well-documented battles with drugs and alcoholism in the past but, despite a recent spell in rehab, it had been widely believed that he was free of his demons. Now it seemed this was not so.

More details began to emerge. The Marin County Sheriff's office had further information. It had received a 911 call at 11.55am Pacific time, it stated, with a man reported to be 'unconscious and not breathing inside his residence'. Robin Williams was pronounced dead at 12.02pm.

The full statement read as follows:

On August 11, 2014, at approximately 11:55 a.m., Marin County Communications received a 9-1-1 telephone call reporting a male adult had been located unconscious and not breathing inside his residence in unincorporated Tiburon, CA. The Sheriff's Office, as well as the Tiburon Fire Department and Southern Marin Fire Protection District were dispatched to the incident with emergency personnel arriving on scene at 12:00 pm. The male subject, pronounced deceased at 12:02 pm, has been identified as Robin McLaurin Williams, a 63-year-old resident of unincorporated Tiburon, CA.

An investigation into the cause, manner, and circumstances of the death is currently underway by the Investigations and Coroner Divisions of the Sheriff's Office. Preliminary information developed during the investigation indicates Mr. Williams was last seen alive at his residence, where he resides with his wife, at approximately 10:00 pm on August 10, 2014. Mr. Williams was located this morning shortly before the 9-1-1 call was placed to Marin County Communications. At this time, the Sheriff's Office Coroner Division suspects the death to be a suicide due to asphyxia, but a comprehensive investigation must be completed before a final determination is made. A forensic examination is currently scheduled for August 12, 2014 with subsequent toxicology testing to be conducted.

The world was reeling but this was nothing compared to Williams' nearest and dearest. 'This morning, I lost my husband and my best friend, while the world lost one of its most beloved artists and beautiful human beings,' said his wife, Susan Schneider. 'I am utterly heartbroken. On behalf of Robin's family, we are asking for privacy during our time of profound grief. As he is remembered, it is our hope the focus will not be on Robin's death, but on the countless moments of joy and laughter he gave to millions.'

And it soon became clear that Robin was anything but in a state of good health. '[He] has been battling severe depression,' said his publicist, Mara Buxbaum. 'This is a tragic and sudden loss. The family respectfully asks for their privacy as they grieve during this very difficult time.' It seemed that his stint in rehab betokened somewhat greater problems than anyone had realised at the time.

Robin's twenty-five-year-old daughter Zelda gave an immensely touching tribute. 'Dad was, is and always will be one of the kindest, most generous, gentlest souls I've ever known, and while there are few things I know for certain right now, one of them is that not just my world, but the entire world is forever a little darker, less colorful and less full of laughter in his absence. We'll just have to work twice as hard to fill it back up again,' she said.

His two sons did likewise. Zack, his eldest, said, 'Yesterday, I lost my father and a best friend and the world got a little grayer. I will carry his heart with me every day. I would ask those that loved him to remember him by being as gentle, kind, and generous as he would be. Seek to bring joy to the world as he sought.'

Cody, twenty-three, added, 'There are no words strong enough to describe the love and respect I have for my father. The world will never be the same without him. I will miss him and take him with me everywhere I go for the rest of my life, and will look forward, forever, to the moment when I get to see him again.'

Fellow comedian David Steinberg had been his manager for thirty-five years. 'Nobody made the world laugh like Robin Williams,' he said. 'My brother, my friend, my soulmate, I will miss you.'

And the tributes were fast to flow in. 'Robin Williams was an airman, a doctor, a genie, a nanny, a president, a professor, a bangarang Peter Pan, and everything in between,' said US President Barack Obama. 'But he was one of a kind. He arrived in our lives as an alien – but he ended up touching every element of the human spirit. He made us laugh. He made us cry. He gave his immeasurable talent freely and generously to those who needed it most – from our troops stationed abroad to the marginalized on our own streets. The Obama family offers our condolences to Robin's family, his friends, and everyone who found their voice and their verse thanks to Robin Williams.'

US Secretary of State John Kerry spoke of his 'extraordinary zest'. 'Robin wasn't just a huge creative genius, but a caring, involved citizen,' he went on. 'I'll always be grateful for his personal friendship and his support for the causes that we both cared about deeply.'

'Robin Williams was a comedy giant, and although we only knew him personally for a season, he was warm, funny and a true professional,' said *The Crazy Ones* production company, 20th Century Fox Television, with whom Robin recently made a television series, *The Crazy Ones*. 'His cast and crew both loved him and loved working with him, and our hearts go out to his family and friends. He was one of a kind.'

David E. Kelley, who was the man behind the show, said, 'The talent was legendary. But equally inspiring, perhaps more so, was his kindness and humanity. A gentle soul who touched us all. A very special man, and our hearts are broken.'

Sarah Michelle Gellar was his co-star. 'My life is a better place because I knew Robin Williams,' she told *People*. 'To my children he was Uncle Robin, to everyone he worked with, he was the best boss anyone had ever known, and to me he was not just an inspiration but he was the father I had always dreamed of having. There are not enough adjectives to describe the light he was, to anyone that ever had the pleasure to meet him. I will miss him every day, but I know the memory of him will live on. And to his family, I thank them for letting us know him and seeing the joy they brought him. Us crazy ones love you.'

CBS, who screened the series, said, 'Our world has lost a comic genius, a gifted actor and a beautiful man. We will remember Robin Williams as one of the unique talents of his time who was loved by many, but also as a kind, caring soul, who treated his colleagues and co-workers with great affection and respect. Our heartfelt thoughts and sympathies go out to his family, loved ones and friends.'

One of Williams' most recent projects was *Night At The Museum: Secret Of The Tomb*, the third film in the popular trilogy, which was made by 20th Century Fox and due to premiere in December 2014. 'There really are no words to describe the loss of Robin Williams,' said the studio in a statement. 'He was immensely talented, a cherished member of our community, and part of the Fox family. Our hearts go out to his family, friends and fans. He will be deeply missed.'

Robin had won numerous accolades, including two SAG (Screen Actors Guild) Awards. Ken Howard, president of SAG-AFTRA, said, 'I am deeply saddened to hear of Robin Williams' death. He was a performer of limitless versatility, equally adept at comedy and drama, whether scripted or improv. With his incomparable manic style, he could appeal to adult sensibilities in a stand-up comedy routine or elicit giggles from children as the voice of Genie in *Aladdin*. Outside of his career, he used his considerable talents to raise money for charity. He was not only a talented man, but a true humanitarian. It's such a tremendous loss.'

Williams had also aired many television specials, including those for Comic Relief, on HBO. 'Robin Williams graced HBO for so many years with his uncommon gifts,' said the network. 'He never failed to elevate his art and did so with a full, generous and loving heart. Always humble and gracious, Robin was a prince and holds a special place in all our hearts.'

A memorial was set up at the Boston Public Garden

bench featured in *Good Will Hunting*. A lifelong fan, Nicholas Rabchenuk and his girlfriend visited it: 'We went to the [Boston] Common and I was really surprised there wasn't anything there,' he told the *Hollywood Reporter*. The couple decided to rectify that: they fetched flowers and chalk and when they came back, they found four fans sitting on the bench and so the quartet decided to write lines from the film. These included 'Sorry guys, I went to see about a girl' and 'Your move, chief'.

That film prompted another tribute and recollection, this time from Minnie Driver, who had also starred in *Good Will Hunting*.

'I'd come to watch him and Matt [Damon] film their beautiful scene on the park bench in *Good Will Hunting*, and when they broke for lunch we sat around on the grass eating sandwiches,' she told the *Hollywood Reporter*. 'What began as a riff on something or other to make us and the crew laugh suddenly extended to office workers out on their lunch break, enjoying the sunshine, and pretty soon he stood up and his big beautiful voice, full of laughter, reached out to the people who were now hurrying down from the street and across the park to catch his impromptu stand-up. There must have been 200 people listening and laughing by the time lunch was over. I just remember how broadly he smiled, patted me on the shoulder and said, "There, now that was GOOD." I loved him, and I will miss him greatly. My thoughts are with his family and friends.'

Similar tributes began to appear elsewhere. At Laugh

Factory on Sunset Boulevard, LA, the marquee read, 'Robin Williams Rest In Peace Make God Laugh'. *Mork & Mindy*, the TV series that had made him famous all those years previously, was set in Boulder, Colorado: fans visited the house to pay tribute. Lights along the Great White Way went dark for a minute, the old tradition whereby Broadway honoured one of its own.

Another co-star was Sally Field, who had appeared with Williams in *Mrs. Doubtfire*. 'I feel stunned and so sad about Robin,' she told *Entertainment Tonight*. 'I'm sad for the world of comedy. And so very sad for his family. And I'm sad for Robin. He always lit up when he was able to make people laugh, and he made them laugh his whole life long... tirelessly. He was one of a kind. There will not be another. Please God, let him now rest in peace.'

He had also starred with Nathan Lane in *The Birdcage*. 'What I will always remember about Robin, perhaps even more than his comic genius, extraordinary talent and astounding intellect, was his huge heart – his tremendous kindness, generosity, and compassion as an acting partner, colleague, and fellow traveler in a difficult world,' said Lane.

Actor Alan Alda spoke of his 'Niagara of wit'. 'I hope it makes us all want to do something,' he wrote on the *TIME.com* website. 'While the whole country, and much of the world, feels this moment of sadness at his death, can we turn the loss of this artist we loved so much into something that pushes back against the ravages of despair?'

Fellow comedian and actor Chevy Chase knew

something of what Williams had been going through. 'Robin and I were great friends, suffering from the same little-known disease: depression,' he said. 'I never could have expected this ending to his life. I cannot believe this. I am overwhelmed with grief.'

Ben Stiller, of course, was also a co-star (*Night At The Museum* franchise) and knew him well. 'A tweet cannot begin to describe the hugeness of Robin Williams' heart and soul and talent,' he wrote. 'This is so sad. #RobinWilliams. I met him when I was 13 and a huge fan and he was so kind and I watched him be kind to every fan i ever saw him with... And with other actors he was so generous and brilliant. He made everyone feel special and equal around him even though he was the genius... His heart was so big and even if you didn't know him, what he gave everyone was that same spirit in his work, so we all felt it... His impact on the world was so positive. He did so much good for people. He made me and so many people laugh so hard for a very long time. And because they don't really tweet, this message represents all the Stillers (Jerry, Anne and Amy) who Robin was a great friend to. Xxxxx'

The Final Cut co-star Mira Sorvino was dreadfully upset. 'I cannot believe we have lost Robin Williams,' she said. 'What a man, what a comedic genius. I counted him among my friends and have such great memories. Robin Williams was sweet and kind and generous and Oh so brilliant, able to incorporate anything and everything into his mind-boggling rants. Robin was a good man and this should not have happened. Devastated. Sending love to his family.'

And from *Old Dogs* co-star John Travolta, 'I've never known a sweeter, brighter, more considerate person than Robin. Robin's commitment as an artist to lifting our mood and making us happy is compared to none. He loved us all and we loved him back.'

An extremely touching tribute came from the family of the late Christopher Reeve. The American actor and Williams had been lifelong friends after meeting when they were both students at the famous Juilliard School in New York, and became so close that they were sometimes described as brothers; after Reeve was paralysed in the wake of a riding accident Robin had been quick to visit and spent a lot of time with his old friend until his untimely death in 2004 (indeed, it was Chris's death that was thought to have knocked him off the wagon in the early noughties). 'After our father's accident, Robin's visit to his hospital room was the first time that Dad truly laughed,' the family said in a statement to *People*. 'Dad later said, "My old friend had helped me know that somehow I was going to be okay."'

Such was the worldwide shock and saturation coverage that, unusually, Lt. Keith Boyd of the Marin County Sheriff's Office held a press conference to tell of the late actor's final moments. He had been found hanged. It emerged that his wife Susan had gone to bed at 10.30pm the previous evening; Robin went to sleep in a separate room and, when she left the house the next morning, she had been under the impression that he was still asleep. She went out at about 10.30am: a neighbour, Sandy Kleinman, saw her go out to walk the dog.

It was actually Mara Buxbaum, Williams' publicist, who first realised something was wrong: when he didn't reply to repeated knocks on the door at around 11.45am, she entered the room and discovered her client. By that time, of course, it was too late. Mara was beside herself: 'The caller [Buxbaum] was distraught and indicated at that time it was an apparent suicide due to a hanging that had taken place and that rigor mortis had set in,' said Boyd. No one would talk about whether there had been a suicide note.

As more details emerged, it became clear that something had been very wrong in recent months. Williams had been sleeping up to eighteen hours a day, spoke of constant tiredness and loss of appetite and had also been quite reclusive. 'His bedroom had blackout curtains, because Robin didn't want light in his bedroom,' a source told *RadarOnline.com*. After his death, pictures emerged of his last public appearance, attending an exhibition at Bay Area Art Gallery. He looked painfully thin, gaunt even, indicating a severe loss of appetite might also have been an issue: another sign of depression. But there was no obvious indication that anything had been wrong. The artist Mark Jaeger, whose work had been on display that night – Robin had purchased a work of his in the past – related that he had appeared to be in good spirits that night, laughing frequently and not drinking. The two discussed possible future projects. But Williams' painfully thin appearance hinted that something really was wrong.

In the aftermath, Jaeger, a ceramics teacher at Marin Catholic High School in Kentfield, was clearly distressed. They had met through Robin's wife Susan, a curator of exhibitions at 142 Throckmorton Theatre, and Williams had been extremely supportive of his work, buying a huge clay head from his 'Superhero' series, which featured ordinary people as superheroes. The two had had a good chat. 'We were actually talking about turning the superhero concept into a movie script,' Jaeger told *Marin Independent Journal*. 'This idea of a superhero homeless person, goes out at night and does good deeds and takes care of people in need. I said, "Robin, I'm enthused. I love the idea that it could be a movie but I don't know how to do that," and he said, "Oh, you just jot down some notes on a piece of paper." And I said, "Then what?" and he said, "Don't worry, I'll take care of it. I'll connect you with the right people and we can go through this process and I'll help you through the process,"' Jaeger said. 'He was so generous. Every time I talked to him, he had such a humility. I'm a nobody, and he made me feel like my work is important.'

Others said that Williams was really not himself. 'The last time I saw Robin was over the weekend, we would catch up on the street, just casual,' a neighbour who did not wish to be named told *Mail Online*. 'He was very drawn and thin, he did not look like the Robin who first moved into this community many years ago. He was a shell of himself, exhausted and not in the best spirits, but still the nice guy I had always known. There seemed to be something on his mind. He was not at all like his stage persona; that was not the Robin I knew. He was more quiet and down-to-earth, not over-the-top, like he was in the movies. He listened well. He was often quiet and very private. The last time I saw him he seemed to be in a bad place emotionally.'

Others also talked about the fact that Robin was much quieter off screen than on and how he used to enjoy walking his dogs in order to be alone with his thoughts. A picture was emerging of a troubled and complex man.

So what could have caused such a dramatic change? Williams' ongoing battles with drink, drugs and depression were now increasingly known but, to the astonishment of many, it now emerged that he might have been experiencing serious financial concerns as well. In some ways this was almost inconceivable – Robin Williams, was a major Hollywood A-lister and had been for decades, with his fortune at one point estimated at £75 million, but he had had two very expensive divorces and, although his name was as famous as ever, the major film roles weren't coming his way in quite the manner they once did. His 600-acre ranch in Napa Valley had been on the market for two years, with the asking price dropped from £21 million to £17.8 million, while he had been telling friends, 'I just can't afford it anymore.'

Indeed, it seemed that the financial difficulties were pretty severe. 'All he could talk about were serious money troubles. Robin was known for being so generous to his friends and family during the height of his success, and would help anyone out that needed it,' a family friend told *Radar Online*. 'There was also frustration that Robin expressed at having to take television and movie roles he didn't want to take, but had to for the pay cheque.'

Stories began to emerge that he was so worried about money that he had even started to sell off his beloved fifty-strong bicycle collection.

Looking at the bigger picture, there were further signs that all was not well. The two divorces were said to have cost £20 million and Williams had talked openly about doing another comedy tour, going back into television and even doing low-budget films. 'The movies are good, but a lot of times they don't even have distribution,' he told *Parade* magazine in 2013 'There are bills to pay. Divorce is expensive. I used to joke they were going to call it "all the money" but they changed it to "alimony". It's ripping your heart out through your wallet.' He was joking – but then again, many a true word is spoken in jest.

By the time of his death, Williams wasn't even living in his ranch: instead he was residing in a bungalow in Tiburon, which he had inherited from his mother Laurie in 2001. He was talking about having to 'downsize' his life: money was clearly on his mind.

Others, however, denied that financial worries had been at the forefront. 'Reports suggesting Robin may have had financial issues are simply false,' his publicist Mara Buxbaum said in an email to *NBC News*. 'I understand people's desire to try to understand this, but we would encourage your focus to be on working to help others and understand depression.' Others equally maintained that the actor had plenty of work in the pipeline and that this was not a cause for concern. Forbes estimated he was still worth the best part of $50 million. Not as much as previously, perhaps, but hardly a man on his uppers.

But then something else came to light; something totally different: not only was poor Robin tormented by a lifetime of demons manifesting themselves in drink and drugs issues, alongside possible money worries and concerns about his career, but he was also in the early stages of a serious illness. It might have been years before it really began to manifest itself but it emerged that Williams had recently been diagnosed with Parkinson's disease. Could this have finally pushed him over the edge?

Opinion was divided but his widow, Susan Schneider, felt that she had to make a statement about an illness her husband had not wanted to go public about and she also wanted to make it clear that he had not succumbed to alcohol again. It read as follows:

Robin spent so much of his life helping others. Whether he was entertaining millions on stage, film or television, our troops on the frontlines, or comforting a sick child – Robin wanted us to laugh and to feel less afraid. Since his passing, all of us who loved Robin

16

have found some solace in the tremendous outpouring of affection and admiration for him from the millions of people whose lives he touched. His greatest legacy, besides his three children, is the joy and happiness he offered to others, particularly to those fighting personal battles.

Robin's sobriety was intact and he was brave as he struggled with his own battles of depression, anxiety as well as early stages of Parkinson's disease, which he was not yet ready to share publicly.

It is our hope in the wake of Robin's tragic passing that others will find the strength to seek the care and support they need to treat whatever battles they are facing so they may feel less afraid.

It was a brave statement to make at a time when Susan was obviously suffering such a terrible loss. However, it did nothing to stop the speculation. Williams had been a keen cyclist, having taken up the sport to help him in the fight against his various addictions. Now his friend, San Francisco bike-shop owner and Robin's biking partner, Tony Tom, who also revealed that Robin had used cycling to keep himself off drugs, wondered whether the A-lister was afraid that, as his disease progressed, he would no longer be able to cycle. Actor and producer Michael J. Fox, meanwhile, himself diagnosed with Parkinson's while still very young, tweeted that he was 'stunned' to hear that Robin Williams had been a fellow sufferer. He was 'pretty sure' that Williams' support for his Michael J. Fox Foundation predated the moment when he found out that he, too, was suffering from the disease, adding, 'A true friend; I wish him peace.'

Now that the news was out, another possibility aired: were the drugs that Williams had been taking to treat his condition actually responsible for pushing him over the edge? Some people certainly thought so. Actor Rob Schneider, with whom Robin had been friends for over twenty years since they both appeared on *Saturday Night Live*, clearly thought so. He tweeted, 'Now that we can talk about it #Robin Williams was on a drug treating the symptoms of Parkinson's. One of the side effects is suicide.'

The family wouldn't be drawn, however, despite rumours that they agreed with this, although a source was prepared to talk. 'Robin had recently left rehab,' he told *Forbes*. 'He was on medication for anxiety and depression and had also started taking drugs to combat the early onset of Parkinson's. Many of these drugs list suicidal thoughts as a possible side effect. A lot of Robin's friends are convinced that the cocktail of prescription pills he was on somehow contributed to his mental state deteriorating as quickly as it did. Robin had always suffered from depression and addiction but the diagnosis and treatment of his Parkinson's was new, as was the combination of drugs he was on.'

Williams had, indeed, always suffered from depression but the Parkinson's diagnosis had made matters much worse, in addition to which it was widely believed that depression is also an early symptom of the disease. Indeed, the revelation attracted so much publicity that the US-based National Parkinson Foundation felt compelled to put out a statement:

> We have all been devastated by Robin Williams' death. We are further saddened to hear that he was recently diagnosed with Parkinson's. While a diagnosis of any serious disease can be overwhelming, Parkinson's and depression can go hand in hand. According to a recent study conducted by NPF, more than half of those with the disease suffer from clinical depression, which is part of the disease process itself. Depression affects quality of life more than the motor impairments of the disease. NPF urges annual screening for depression as a critical part to treating Parkinson's. Treatment for depression should include both medications and counseling. The National Parkinson Foundation encourages people living with Parkinson's and their families to seek expert care from a neurologist.

The reverberations continued. Susan, poleaxed by grief, left the marital home and the community where they lived together. Williams' children continued to express bewilderment and upset.

Zelda tweeted a quote from the French novel *The Little Prince* by Antoine De Saint-Exupéry:

You – you alone will have the stars as no one else has them… In one of the stars I shall be living. In one of them I shall be laughing. And so it will be as if all the stars were laughing, when you look at the sky at night, you – only you – will have stars that can laugh. I love you. I miss you. I'll try to keep looking up. – Z

It emerged that the funeral had been held very quickly: an Episcopalian service, the religion that Williams had been brought up in, at Monte's Chapel of the Hills, a funeral home in San Anselmo, California. After the private service, Robin's ashes were scattered in the San Francisco Bay – appropriate, for he had lived there for much of his life since his late teens. As those close to him continued to struggle to make sense of what had happened, there was increased speculation that it had been a spur-of-the-moment decision, with a close associate saying that just days before he had been talking about upcoming projects. He had been 'completely engaged in the conversation', the source told *TMZ* and, as such, certainly didn't seem to be harbouring any thoughts about leaving. But then again, it was perhaps not widely appreciated that Williams had had a traumatic childhood, which left him scarred for the rest of his life. He'd played many damaged characters so magnificently because he himself was one too and, perhaps finally, he was no longer able to hold out against the despair that had appeared at periodic intervals throughout the course of his life.

A MUCH-LOVED MAN

A genuine tide of grief was developing: Robin Williams may have been flawed but he was a decent, kind and caring man and his untimely demise was not only affecting his fans but also those who had previously never given him much thought. So who, exactly, was Robin Williams? And how had he come to make such a huge impact on so many people all around the world?

'Death is nature's way of saying, "Your table's ready."'
ROBIN WILLIAMS

CHAPTER TWO

OH, WHAT A LONELY BOY

*'Comedy can be a cathartic way to
deal with personal trauma.'*
ROBIN WILLIAMS

Chicago, Illinois. It was the height of summer in the Windy City and Laura McLaurin, a former model from Jackson, Mississippi, and her husband, Robert Fitzgerald Williams, an executive at the Ford Motor Company, were elated. On 21 July 1951, Robin McLaurin Williams was born. He had two elder half-brothers, Robert Todd Williams (who was to become a wine-maker known as 'Toad') from his father's first marriage and McLaurin Smith-Williams from his mother's first marriage but, essentially, although he always got on very well with his half-brothers, Robin was an only child; they all were. 'All three of us grew up as only children – Todd, myself and Robin. I was adopted by my mother's parents after her divorce from her first marriage. Todd grew up with his mother. We all get along famously. Todd is no blood relation to me, but we're real close,' McLaurin, a physics teacher, told the *Chicago Tribune* in 1991.

For someone who was to develop such an anarchic character, Williams certainly came from highly respectable stock: his mother's great grandfather was the Mississippi senator and governor Anselm J. McLaurin, while his father hailed from an extremely prominent family in Evansville, Indiana. There was great wealth there: Robert's father, also called Robert, and originally from Kentucky, was the chief clerk and in 1902 was secretary, treasurer and general manager of the Indiana Tie Company. 'He has contributed much to the success of the enterprise, capably controlling the interests of the company and managing its trade connections in such a manner that successful results are achieved,' according to the History of the City of Evansville and Vanderburgh County, Indiana. Quite a few of Williams' family members are buried in the Evansville cemetery, a fact that caused much excitement when it was revealed by Robin Williams' Evansville fans.

But that wasn't all. Famously, Robin could list English, Welsh, Irish, Scottish, German and French among his ancestry: a clue, perhaps, as to why he was so good at accents in later life. The family was wealthy: Robin grew up surrounded by privilege and creature comforts but, in many other ways, his was a deprived upbringing. His father was forty-six when Robin was born. He was strict and didn't have a lot of time for his young son. Robin's mother was an aspiring model who had many philanthropic interests outside the home. She, too, was largely absent and already wounds were beginning to form when he was very young that would never heal. Over time they would grow into torments, provoking a good deal of anguish for the rest of his life.

Robin's early life was spent in Lake Forest, an affluent suburb north of Chicago. In those days he was nothing like the outgoing comic he was to become. The family had a vast house but he spent a great deal of time on his own, playing with his toys: his father was often away because of business, while his mother was involved in charitable work. It does not take a degree in psychiatry to work out that the young Robin spent a great deal of his time trying and failing to catch the attention of his parents – something that was to turn into a lifelong quest.

Shy, plump, melancholic and quiet, he was also a nervous child, afraid of the shadows and somewhat afraid of his father, come to that. It may be a cliché to point out that so many people become comedians to combat their own inner melancholy but Williams' childhood was a classic example of what turns an individual to blot their inner pain with drink and drugs and a lot of comedy. Laughter, as a child, was often in short supply. 'I collected model soldiers, thousands of them,' he recalled. 'You learn how to create games for yourself and you read a lot. It wasn't exactly fun, but later on it helps with your range as a comedian and it gives you an imagination.'

Nevertheless, he did have some friends and one such friend remembers his vast collection of toys – 2,000 in all. 'I just had the regular, olive green plastic army men, but Robin had this whole setup of hand-painted English soldiers made of lead,' Jeff Hodgen, who met Williams in fifth grade at Lake Forest's Gorton Elementary School, told the *Chicago Tribune*. 'He was kind of standoffish when we first met, but that was only because he was the new kid at school. I remember once we were throwing snowballs, and we hit a cop car, which put a stop to that. Every time one of our phones rang at home for months after, we were terrified it was the police calling to talk to our parents.' Interestingly, Hodgen added that Williams was not at all the clown of the class; rather a serious and somewhat introverted boy.

Life in Lake Forest was good, however. Despite the proximity to Chicago, it was more like a small city in its own right: part of the north shore development, it had Lake Michigan on one side, where the town's inhabitants could go swimming in the very hot summers and ice skating in freezing-cold winters. The large houses, standing in their own plots of land, were in many cases designed by some of the twentieth century's most famous architects, including David Adler and Frank Lloyd Wright; the big gardens were good for playing in and children could cycle down the city's wide sidewalks, as they were expected to do – there was no cycling on the quiet roads. Poverty was not much of an issue in Lake Forest and neither were ethnic minorities: the city was largely white.

After Gorton, Robin moved to Deer Path Junior High School in the sixth grade but, when he was in seventh grade, aged about twelve, the family moved to Detroit. Hodgen was surprised but accepted it. 'I missed him but I had just started playing football, so I sucked it up,' he said.

The family moved to a huge, thirty-room mansion in Bloomfield Hills at the corner of Woodward and Long Lake and, in later years, Robin made it sound like paradise. 'It was a giant, beautiful old mansion, with a gatehouse, an empty garage with room for 25 cars, barns, and there was a very wonderful old English man, Mr. Williams, who looked after the gardens,' he told the *Detroit Free Press*. 'We didn't own it; we just rented it. Then we moved to Chicago, and when we came back to Detroit a few years later, we just lived in an apartment. And it was very different, you know. But the first house, it was so wonderful, so peaceful. There was no one for miles around. Only this giant golf course with people named Tad whacking the old ball.'

In actual fact, this was Robin embroidering the tale, whether deliberately or not, for the truth is somewhat less rosy. Surrounded by his giant toy collection, he had a whole floor to himself in the attic but he didn't enjoy it. He was rather frightened of the shadows and dark corners. It was a solitary existence for a little boy and, as Robin played on his own, he started to make up stories and characters. At that stage no one had a clue that they had a comic genius in their midst, however: all they saw was a little boy wanting to be loved, having been uprooted from a previous existence and now starting over from scratch. 'My only companions, my only friends as a child, were my imagination,' he once said.

Church was a part of his life. His mother was a Christian Scientist, although Robin was brought up as an Episcopalian. Indeed, he played a very active role in the church for a time and it, too, would become the source of some of his comedy, as well as the inspiration when he starred in the 2007 film *License to Wed*. 'Having been a choirboy, and I'm not Catholic, just going back to the old days when I was into going to church and remembering, as a Protestant, which is Catholic light once again, the idea of somebody that could really advise and has something [to] offer,' he told *Canmag* around the time of the movie's launch. 'It was just remembering those guys that I grew up with in the Episcopal Church, which is there is no purgatory, just spiritual escrow. That was [the] beginning of that. And then the idea that he's pretty much hands on as much as you can be without being a priest.'

Robin enrolled at Detroit Country Day School, a private school where he did well in some respects but also had some very unhappy times. He became president of the class, played soccer and joined the wrestling team, and one of his teachers is said to have been the person upon whom he based his role as John Keating in *Dead Poets Society*, loved school, maybe too much really,' he told the *Washington Post* in an interview that coincided with the release of *Jack* (1996), a film about a boy who ages four times faster than everyone else and which painted a much sunnier picture of his early days than was the reality.

'I was summa cum laude in high school. I was driven that way. I can't say it was easy to fit in. I just went out of my way to fit in. It was a private boys' school, Detroit Country Day, and I played soccer. I was on the wrestling team. Mr. All-Around, you know? But I think what made me want to play Jack was that innocent time before all that, riding bikes, friends in treehouses, all those things that loom on the boundaries of child and boy. When you're ten, you are still a boy, and that time right before puberty, which hits at twelve – or eleven if you live somewhere the milk is different – is so incredible. A boy is still so vulnerable then. Boys that age don't have a lot of chops in terms of hiding feelings. What they feel is right there on their faces.'

In fact, what some of those boys felt was malevolence. Robin might have loved school, or at least he had come to think he did, but he had a fair few problems to deal with when he was there and it was this, combined with seeking out his mother's attention and his relative isolation in the family home, that really began to lay down the foundations for the comedian he would one day become. In another interview, this time with the *Oklahoman* in 1991, he gave a considerably more subdued description of life back then.

'I wasn't so exuberant,' he said. 'I spent about three years in an all-boys school. It was almost like the one in *Dead Poets Society*. Blazer. Latin motto. I was getting pushed around a lot. Not only was there, like, physical bullying but there was intellectual bullying going on. It made me toughen up, but it also made me pull back a lot. I had a certain reticence about dealing with people. Through comedy, I found a way to bridge the gap…'

In other words, he was being bullied. To start with, he tried to find other routes to go home but that didn't work. Boys taunted him because he was, as they saw it, small, fat and well spoken. He was also dyslexic, which meant he struggled at school and, in all likelihood, suffered from Attention Deficit Disorder (ADHD), neither of which conditions were recognised back then. Robin couldn't fight back physically, nor could he get away from his fellow pupils, so instead he tried a distraction technique: he began trying to make them laugh. 'I started telling jokes as a way to stop the shit getting kicked out of me,' he once revealed, again a textbook example of the melancholia that hides behind so many comedians' smiles. Using laughter to avert violence? Right from the start Williams must surely have known his talents would prove a double-edged sword.

Nor were bullies the only people Robin was trying to impress. He wanted to fit in at school but at home he continued to long for the attention of his parents, particularly his mother. And so he employed exactly the same trick as he did at school: he told jokes.

'I'm just beginning to realize that it wasn't always that happy,' Williams admitted in an interview with *Esquire Magazine*. 'My childhood was kind of lonely. Quiet. My father was away; my mother was working, doing benefits. I was basically raised by this maid, and my mother would come in later, you know, and I knew her and she was wonderful and charming and witty. But I think maybe comedy was part of my way of connecting with my mother – "I'll make Mommy laugh and that will be okay" – and that's where it started.' In fact, his first-ever impression was of his grandmother; the start of a talent that was to define him.

And so it went on, the little boy desperate to avoid being beaten at school and, at home, eager for parental attention. And as he continued to develop coping strategies, he was beginning to discover that he really did have the most phenomenal ability to make people laugh. But it never entirely worked: the family had maids who looked after Robin but, as fond of them as he might have been, they were no substitute for his mother. As an adult, he confessed to an acute fear of abandonment and a severe case of 'Love Me Syndrome'. It wasn't hard to work out why. Despite having some friends, his was a childhood spent in loneliness and isolation. The man who would one day have the whole world eating out of his hand was a shy, lonely and frightened little boy and, at the heart of it, that is what Robin Williams always remained. As someone once observed, all the money and success in life cannot make up for an unhappy childhood.

Nor did his mother's religion help, although, typically, he turned it into a subject for humour. He was attacked 'because my mother was a Christian Dior Scientist. I was not only picked on physically but intellectually – people used to kick copies of George Sand in my face.' It was a brave attempt to hide past pain but the sadness still shone through.

When Robin was about sixteen there was still more upheaval, although this was to prove the making of him. Increasingly disillusioned with the automobile industry, his father Robert took early retirement and the family moved again, this time to Woodacre, California, part of Marin County, an area Robin was to make his home for much of his life. He enrolled at Redwood High School in Larkspur. Unlike the previous establishment, this was not a private school and it opened him up to a whole new world. Hawaiian shirts became a part of his wardrobe (and remained there); he started driving a Land Rover... Life opened up.

'When I came out to California to go to high school, it was 1969,' he told the *Oklahoman*. 'I went to this gestalt high school, where one of the teachers actually took LSD one day. So you walked in and you hear [whispers], "I'm Lincoln."' The place suited his anarchic personality perfectly: from the formalities of the Midwest to California just after the Summer of Love was quite an eye-opener. And by now his joke-telling was such that he was seriously beginning to consider a career in the performing arts.

Indeed, the move from the Midwest was probably the making of him. The Midwest still seems to be dominated by pioneer thinking – it is only just over a century since men risked their lives to bring the territory under control. But laid-back California and San Francisco was something else altogether. In later life Williams enjoyed living there because no one seemed to notice him, he said. Of course, this was partly because he was a long-term local resident and they were used to him but it also implied that there were already so many inhabitants who were, perhaps, a little eccentric in that area that he fitted right in.

And the same applied to his considerably more relaxed school, where he was away from the tormentors and able to enjoy himself at last. And while it might not have been a private establishment, it was still a sound place to study, with plenty of other alumni going on to make their names. Comedian and author Greg Behrendt was one such pupil, as was the actor David Dukes. Pulitzer Prize-winning journalist for the *New York Times* Eric Schmitt was another, as was Andy Luckey, who went on to produce the television version of *Teenage Mutant Ninja Turtles*. There were some noted academics too, including Gunnar Carlsson, a professor of mathematics at Stanford University, and noted US epidemiologist Don Francis, who became a big name in HIV and AIDS research.

From the moment he first saw it, Williams' new city made an impact on him. 'I was sixteen years old,' he told *American Way* magazine in 2007. 'My father and mother [and I] had driven across the country. As we drove across the Golden Gate Bridge, there was actually fog pouring in.

I'd never seen fog in my life. Is that poison gas? No. The way it pours over the hills in Marin County and comes over the Gate – it's quite impressive. That was my first impression – what is this strange smoke?! But it was quite beautiful, seeing the bridge. In Detroit, there aren't many things that are that big. I was also struck that quite close to the city, there's all this nature. Mount Tamalpais State Park. We have the whole coastline – extraordinarily beautiful.'

All in all, it was a new environment that was a welcome change and brought him the opportunity to mature into the man he wanted to be; to explore sport and drama and also to relax. His father, of whom he had always been a little afraid, may have become more relaxed too. He was retired now, after all, out of the world of commerce and able to relax in the domestic environment in a way he never really had before. (That said, Williams never really spoke a great deal about his father, other than to recall the time when he launched into him for buying a Japanese car rather than an American one. So perhaps relaxation never came.)

His mother Laurie certainly noticed the change in her son. 'Robin was very shy as a child,' she told the *Chicago Tribune*. 'His father was strict, and I think the turning point for Robin came when he left Detroit Country Day School, which was a bunch of boys wearing very proper white shirts, and we moved to Marin. He went to Redwood High School and began bringing home some pretty wild and wooly friends. I don't think they would have been drawn to him if he hadn't been pretty wild himself. Later, his exposure to improvisation with the Committee [an improvisational comedy troupe] was very exciting for him. People would call out a single line, and he was very good at improvising from just that.'

She was certainly aware of just how talented her son was, even if she never entirely realised that a great deal of it was to impress her. Ultimately, the lonely boy putting on an impression of his grandmother to make his mother laugh morphed into an international star and she was certainly proud of that. 'I feel Robin was put on Earth to make us laugh,' she continued. 'You know, at the Yale Drama School, I'm told they use Robin and Steve Martin as perfect examples of the fool in a king's court. The fool has to be brilliant, well informed and able to make the king laugh without getting his head chopped off. That's Robin.'

And it was: for he was to become the Court Jester, pricking the pomposity of the great and good but, somehow, always getting away with it. It should not be forgotten that not only did Williams have enormous talent but he possessed great charm too. Even at his most manic there was never a sense that he was going out to wound anyone with his comedy: if anything, the only person he appeared to be intending to hurt was himself. And all that stemmed back to the loneliness of his earliest years – he himself had been badly hurt himself and, somehow, that hurt never went away.

But he was much happier now than previously, racketing about a big mansion on his own. 'We lived in Tiburon, in this little house,' he told *American Way* magazine. 'There's a great restaurant in Tiburon called Sam's Anchor Cafe, which is still there. It's a seafood restaurant that my father liked because you can sit outside, on the warm days, or inside. It's just an old-school seafood-and-hamburger place, and my father loved the hamburgers.'

But strangely, in Robin's relationship with his mother, the humour remained, at some level, attached to childhood. Although the rest of the world saw him on adult terms, the relationship between mother and child never really develops from being exactly that and, although Williams had now grown up, he still operated on some fundamental level with his mother as if he was still small.

'He's very good at voices, you know,' she continued. 'He can do a little child very well. Sometimes, I'll be rushing to get out of the house, and I'll get this call [little girl's voice]: "Hello, this is Candy. My mommy isn't home. Can I come over and play with you?" And I get very impatient; he still can fool me. He also has a key to my house, and sometimes I'll call, and he'll answer the phone and impersonate the help, telling me that Mrs. Williams has moved away.'

This does not sound entirely healthy. Indeed, Robin would never break away from the difficulties of early childhood and this compulsion to make his mother laugh, although he certainly had her attention in later years. But back in high school, no longer plagued by bullies as he had been earlier, he was beginning to blossom. He kept up with the athletics – for a short time he even contemplated going professional and excelled as a runner, another pastime that ended up in his stand-up act when he compared the famous 'runners' high' to getting high on drugs – joined the drama club and began to find his feet. Sharp-witted as ever, by now there was no need to try and outwit the bullies but he couldn't stop himself from trying to amuse his fellow pupils anyway. As for the acting, in later life he claimed he'd only taken it up in order to get laid.

(This was more mythologising on his part: he also once told the British TV presenter and chat-show host Michael Parkinson that he decided to become an actor after seeing the film *Dr. Strangelove: How I Learned To Stop Worrying And Love The Bomb*. Strangely enough, that film starred Peter Sellers, who had the same ability to mimic and transform himself into a multitude of different characters before your very eyes. Another early influence was *2001: A Space Odyssey*, which his parents took him to see.)

Williams was hardly your average jock though. After his death, a fellow schoolmate was asked if it was true that he used to start every day with the cry, 'Good morning, Redwood High!' (an unlikely scenario, it must be said). His schoolmate's verdict was a little blunt: 'No way. C'mon. Nobody does stuff like that. That guy was such a geek. He wore bow ties and was super-quiet. I never liked him.'

But other people did. He really did have friends now – people he could hang out with – and soon he was about to start meeting others with whom he would remain friends for the rest of his life. William Drew met Williams at Redwood High School in 1967. 'I remember Rob and

I walking a cool-down lap after track practice,' he told the BBC in the aftermath of his death. 'As we passed the shot putters, Rob suddenly stopped, walked over to the pit, looked over the three massive guys that were tossing the shot, picked up one of the heavy steel balls, and, well, use your imagination on the comment that came forth from the mouth of Robin Williams. Same in Drama Club – no script was safe, no line sacred. Two words summarise Robin: passion and compassion. He was focused and passionate about everything he did, and, as he demonstrated in his later years, was compassionate about others.'

But it was time to move on, to start thinking about the future and decide what to do next. Although Williams had survived an admittedly tough childhood, in his late teens he was coming into his own, already exceptionally witty and adept at making people laugh. But it wasn't yet entirely clear that this would be the making of him, not only as an individual, but also as a performer. His classmates couldn't quite fathom what to make of it all. Would he make it out there in the big, wide world in whatever capacity? On graduation, his fellow students voted him both 'funniest' and 'least likely to succeed' – they were certainly wrong there.

'And some people say Jesus wasn't Jewish. OF COURSE he was Jewish! 30 years old, single, lives with his parents, come on! He works in his father's business, his mom thought he was God's gift. He's Jewish! Give it up!'

ROBIN WILLIAMS

CHAPTER THREE

ROBIN AND THE JUILLIARD

*'I'm a born entertainer. When I open the fridge door and
the light goes on, I burst into song.'*
ROBIN WILLIAMS

Robin Williams was, if not a born showman, then one who
had certainly tuned into his talents by the vicissitudes of
his childhood. But the penny had still not quite dropped.
And so it was that in 1969 he enrolled at Claremont Men's
College in Claremont, California, to study political science.
But it was not what he was meant to be doing and it didn't
last. In fact, he was there for one semester: depending on
who you believe, he either dropped out because he realised
he'd made a bad mistake or he was expelled for crashing a
golf cart into the dining hall. He had certainly done some
acting in his time there and was increasingly called on to
follow that particular star. Whatever the truth, he didn't last.

His father wasn't thrilled but took it as well as might be expected. He did, however, advise his son to learn a practical trade, just to be on the safe side – welding. Robin did actually take a class but his instructor wasn't very encouraging: 'You can go blind from this,' he told him. It was not the happiest moment.

In truth, to anyone with a grain of perception it was increasingly obvious that Robin wasn't just talented, he was extraordinary; he totally stood apart. Even now, at this early stage in his career, he was displaying a wit, an ability to improvise, a comedic gift extraordinary in one so young. All those early elements – the fight against bullying, trying to attract his mother's attention, the loneliness which led him to depend on his imagination – were there, of course, but there was something more. Williams had quite exceptional qualities and these were now beginning to come through.

Claremont Men's College and a career in political science was not an option. A rethink was called for, and fast. And so he found himself at the College of Marin, in Kentfield, California, where he was to study drama for the next three years. It was a community college, where students did not exactly receive degrees per se but undertook the type of studies that were essentially somewhere between school and university. Now his anarchic side was seriously unleashed. Fellow students remember him walking around in green shorts and a swimming cap, doing silly walks. (This was around the time that Monty Python would have been on British television and many an aspiring comedian was doing silly walks of his own.)

According to his drama professor, James Dunn, right from the start he stood out. It was a character in a Dickens' adaptation that marked him out, and quickly too. And as the years went by it was his talent for improvisation that truly set him apart. 'I first knew he was more talented than the other kids when he played Fagin in *Oliver!*' Dunn told *Marin Independent Journal* shortly after Williams' death was announced. 'We were having light board issues and by midnight had only made it through half the musical. At one point he started talking to a baton he was carrying, and the baton talked back. It cut the tension and he had people laughing in hysterics. I remember calling my wife at 2 a.m. and telling her that this young man was going to be something special.'

Fagin wasn't the only role in which he stood out: friends also remember his Malvolio from Shakespeare's *Twelfth Night*. Critics who felt that he should have stayed in stand-up comedy and not gone into serious acting might be surprised to learn the acting ambition was there from the start. Then again, Williams would take the famous soliloquies and use them as inspiration for some extended improvisation of his own. He reduced fellow students to tears of laughter, although, despite his subsequent comments about his former pupil, many felt that Dunn's patience was tested just a little at times. However, he did appreciate the phenomenal energy that flowed out of his student, not least when it manifested itself in the early hours. Dunn ran an annual twenty-four hour fundraiser, putting his students on in different capacities. No matter how late it was, Robin would turn up at 2am or 3am and launch into his performance.

Indeed, whenever he was on public display, he did not stop. He had a little Volkswagen Beetle, which he would drive to the Trident restaurant on Sausalito wharf. To supplement his studies, he worked there as a waiter and even there he would lay on a sideshow, juggling with plates and glasses and whatever came to hand while treating the diners to an impromptu comedy routine. Marin had never seen the like! Off duty, he was not at all similar though, for he was shy. In the aftermath of his death many commented that, when he was off stage, he was quite different to on stage: not a joker and, in many ways, quite withdrawn. A friend said that Robin lived 'in a dark place' and back then this was also true.

But that didn't stop him from working on his act. When he wasn't attending college or working as a waiter, Williams was starting to do the rounds of the local comedy clubs, beginning with Holy City Zoo, where he worked his way up from being a bartender to actually getting on the stage. Holy City Zoo gets its name from its first owner, Robert Steger, who took possession of a sign for free at a closing-down sale at a zoo in Holy City, California. (It was once said Williams 'used the club as his neighbourhood rehearsal space'.) Located in the Richmond area of San Francisco, it was a tiny space, seating just seventy-eight, selling beer, wine and soft drinks, and was originally a folk music club. However, the management began holding open-mic nights for comedians on Sundays, which eventually became so popular that they were extended to the rest of the week.

This was where Robin could begin honing his craft, in a safe, small environment, among the kind of people he knew. He had a considerably longer history of formal study behind him than most people realised, but this, and other San Francisco comedy clubs, was where he really learned his trade. (Indeed, after he became famous, he returned to Holy City Zoo, although he was always at pains to let the other performers go on before him. Just as well... He would have been quite an act to follow.)

Holy City Zoo first shut down in 1984, although it was to open its doors again. 'I'm sad,' said Robin. 'We had wonderful times here, strange times here; this wasn't a haven, it was a game preserve. I remember a big black guy who'd come in with a baseball bat and say, "I'd like to audition." But a lot of that is in the past. So many changes.'

When the club finally shut down for good in 1993, he was as depressed as many of its former alumni: it was 'like someone pulling life support on your aunt. It's depressing. The Zoo was the womb.'

The comedian Steve Pearl saw Williams performing there. He was a 'tornado, frenetic and ripping all over the stage,' Pearl told *The New Yorker* in a tribute to Williams. 'It inspired and scared me at the same time.' By now, he was also beginning to earn some money of his own. Throughout his lifetime he was renowned for his exceptional generosity and it was there right at the beginning, when he was earning virtually nothing while working at Holy City Zoo, that he became aware of a friend's gambling debt. He paid it off.

Other places he appeared included The Boarding House and the Old Spaghetti Factory. The Boarding House was another comedy hotspot: it was where Steve Martin recorded his first three albums and was also host to various music legends, including Dolly Parton and Talking Heads. The Old Spaghetti Factory started as exactly that – a pasta factory – until it was converted into a restaurant that also offered up cabaret. It, too, played host to some extremely famous names, among them pioneers of the Beat generation Jack Kerouac and Allen Ginsberg; also Ken Kesey (author of *One Flew Over the Cuckoo's Nest*). The whole scene was incredibly lively and Williams was a major part of it. By now he was beginning to build up a following: audiences were seeking out the gigs where he would perform. Almost certainly he didn't really need what was to come next, as he was doing so well that he was very much on his way to success, but the young Robin was full of ambition and eager to attend one of the best performing-arts schools of all.

It was already apparent that he was going places but now he stepped into the big league. After three years at Marin he won himself a full scholarship to The Juilliard School in New York in 1973. He was one of only twenty students to win a place that year and one of just two to be accepted into the Advanced Programme by John Houseman, who was really the first person to spot his full potential. The other student was Christopher Reeve of *Superman* fame, who would become a lifelong friend. Another classmate was the American stage and film actor William Hurt. 'He wore tie-dyed shirts with tracksuit bottoms and talked a mile a minute,' Reeve later recalled of his friend. 'I'd never seen so much energy contained in one person. He was like an untied balloon that had been inflated and immediately released. I watched in awe as he virtually caromed off the walls of the classrooms and hallways. To say that he was "on" would be a major understatement.'

This marked a significant step forward in Williams' fortunes. The Juilliard is one of the most prestigious performing-arts schools in the world. Based in the Lincoln Center for Performing Arts in New York, it is extremely difficult to get into and boasts as its alumni a significant proportion of the crème de la crème of the American performing industry. Dance, drama and music were all taught there and to land a place was to be as assured as anyone could be in the fickle showbiz world that you were cut out to be a success.

The Juilliard, although a school for actors, not comedians, contributed hugely to Robin's future comedy. He had already come from an educated, wealthy and sophisticated background but The Juilliard gave him an extra layer of education, reference and knowledge. Because Williams could be so manic on stage and also because he got involved in the 1970s drugs scene and was so very much a part of our pop culture, it is easy to overlook quite how well educated and widely read he was. Already he knew Shakespeare but The Juilliard taught him much more: he was a man who could spout at length a Shakespearian soliloquy before veering off at a tangent and talking about drugs. The snootiness in some quarters about his mainstream acting career was totally misplaced: Williams was a classically trained, highly educated actor – he just happened to have a manic side as well.

After he joined The Juilliard he came to the attention of John Houseman, the Romanian-born British-American actor who had previously worked extensively with Orson Welles and was widely acclaimed for the role of Professor Charles Kingsfield in the 1973 film *The Paper Chase*. A titan of the performing arts world, both in the cinema and theatre, he was also the founding director of the Drama Division at The Juilliard and his other protégés included the actor and comedian Kevin Kline, actress and singer Patti LuPone and actor, tenor, voice artist and comedienne Mandy Patinkin. Williams' experiences at The Juilliard would prove to be somewhat mixed, of which more below, but he undoubtedly benefited from his work with Houseman.

While at The Juilliard, he and Christopher Reeve shared a room and it was here that they developed a bond that ended only with Christopher's sad and premature death from cardiac arrest in 2004. Indeed, Robin couldn't have spoken more highly of his friend: 'He is SO good, and such a method actor, that Oliver Sacks wanted to hook him up to an EEG to see if he actually duplicated the brainwaves of the actual patients. No joke,' he said in an interview with *Reddit* that appeared in 2013. 'Him being such a great friend to me at Juilliard, literally feeding me because I don't think I literally had money for food or my student loan hadn't come in yet, and he would share his food with me.' The two young men pledged whichever one of them became the more successful, he would help the other. In the event, both became successful around the same time but the bond endured, with Williams continuing to play an enormous role in Reeve's life after his tragic riding accident. It was rumoured that he supported the family financially – perhaps a small return for all that shared food.

Other classmates included Kelsey Grammer (of *Cheers* and *Frasier* fame) and the actress Diane Venora, who earned a Golden Globe nomination and New York Film Critics Award for her performance in Clint Eastwood's *Bird*, a portrait of jazz great Charlie Parker. 'We were in the same class for four years,' Diane told the *Los Angeles Times*. 'He was brilliant and complex, deeply sensitive, possessing a vulnerability and humility that gave his work tremendous power. I loved him very much.'

Christopher Reeve also spoke very highly of his friend's emerging talent. 'Robin and I came in at the third year level,' he told *New York Magazine* in 1993. 'We were put in special advanced sections; often, we were the only students in a class. John Houseman had an idea of what the Juilliard actor should be – well spoken but a bit homogenized – so it's not surprising the teachers were thrown by Robin. He did a monologue from *Beyond the Fringe* that made us laugh so hard we were in physical pain; they said it was "a comedy bit, not acting".'

But Robin was extremely good at the 'comedy bit' and he just kept getting better. Robert M. Beseda, who became assistant dean of drama at North Carolina School of the Arts, was a peer. 'We were classmates,' he told *Time Warner Cable News*. 'He was one year behind me. I didn't know him well; he was too cool for the likes of me, but he was so funny. He held court and kept us all in stitches. I remember him in a workshop of *A Midsummer Night's Dream*. He was Thisbe and when the Mechanicals performed their play in Act V, he had two grapefruits down his dress as breasts. At one point they popped out suddenly and he began to juggle them. It was one of the funniest sight gags in the history of comedy. I will never forget it. He is a great loss to a world that needs what he gave us so generously!'

New York, meanwhile, was in sharp contrast to San Francisco. The laid-back city on the Pacific was nothing like the teeming metropolis where Williams now lived, home to Broadway, where he would later perform, and one of the most vibrant and exciting places in the world. It was the first time he had lived on his own as an adult (albeit rooming with Reeve) and the first time he was free of his parents and able to live on his own terms, but the old demons remained.

People were fascinated by his comedy – by the manic element in it – but none of them would have truly understood what lay behind it: the bullied boy reaching out to an absentee mother. He was learning to grow a shell and disguise the hurt by channelling it elsewhere but even the excitement of The Juilliard and New York City could never completely erase the pain. Ominously, it would not be long before he sought other ways of blotting it out but, for now, he was learning fast. In order to make some money, he and a friend did a white-faced mime sequence in front of the Metropolitan Museum of Art, one day earning themselves $75 – quite a decent amount back then.

One of Robin (and Christopher's) teachers was Edith Skinner, a leading voice and speech coach, who taught them how to speak in different dialects. She soon discovered that Robin could already do so, with no outside help. Michael Kahn was another teacher and, while somewhat dismissive of him as a mere stand-up comic, he was won round after seeing his performance as a young man in Tennessee Williams' *The Night of the Iguana*, which turned into a great success.

Williams continued at The Juilliard for another two years, eventually leaving without actually graduating. Again, stories differ as to why. Some decades back, he could be somewhat diffident about the reason for his departure. According to some versions of the event, he dropped out of his own accord – again. But in the book *Juilliard: A History*, author Andrea Olmstead recounts that the school told him to leave, although she did include this in a list of 'blunders that would eventually embarrass the school'. Indeed, The Juilliard has made a great play of talking up the association with Robin Williams and, whatever they might have thought at the time, certainly became pretty proud of the association. He himself never cast a great deal of light on the subject, saying in 2001 that 'he has no degrees from any colleges yet'. (The Juilliard went on to award him an honorary degree.) But it seems as if The Juilliard significantly underestimated him, seeing him as a comic rather than an actor, and failed to spot the depths below.

Gerald Freedman, dean emeritus of the School of Drama at North Carolina School of the Arts in downtown Winston-Salem, was Williams' teacher at The Julliard and an interview he gave after Robin's death may cast further light on the subject. 'This is beyond sad... He was a genius, out of the box... I was his teacher at Juilliard,' he told *Time Warner Cable News*. 'He was not a very good fit for a conservative, classical training program, but we recognized his talent and he was a good sport about it. No one was surprised when he left school before he graduated and became what he became. I am so sorry we have lost him, that it came to this. He had so much to say about the world we live in. Perhaps it all got to him. I don't know.'

Good sport? This would certainly imply that his departure was not entirely of his own choosing but an inability to control his own sense of anarchy, plus the fact that he had to turn every performance into a comic turn was, again, the sign of an actual need within him. He himself once admitted that he suffered from 'Love Me' syndrome and there it was, manifesting itself again.

Robert M. Beseda also hinted that Williams' temperament was simply unsuited to formal study. 'He was a great mimic – he could mimic all the teachers like dead on and maybe they didn't like that,' he told *News Piedmont*. It was certainly one of life's ironies that very many students who went on to study at The Juilliard cited Robin Williams as one of their heroes and one of the reasons they were inspired to act. It also implied that he could be somewhat tactless in challenging the authority figures. And the authority figures didn't like that.

A third version of events has since emerged – it must be said a considerably later one and one that, perhaps, resembles some face saving – on the part of The Juilliard. It has been said that none other than John Houseman suggested Williams should leave on the grounds that there was nothing more The Juilliard could teach him and so he might as well start earning his comedy credential straight away. This doesn't entirely ring true – The Juilliard is the sort of place that always believes it can teach people something more. But Williams, uncharacteristically, remained silent. Clearly he never felt the need to give his own side of the story, preferring to let it rest.

The actor James Marsters, who appeared as Spike in the TV series *Buffy The Vampire Slayer* (1997–2003) and who also left The Juilliard early, gave another insight. 'The joke about Juilliard is the only actors that end up working are the ones that get kicked out,' he told *Mediatainement Online* in 2001. 'Robin Williams, John Hurt – the list is endless of people who were told they would never be actors, that they should get out of the business before they become bitter. Juilliard is a heavily regimented acting program and if you have a spirit which is individual, they will try and kick that out of you. And my opinion is that my instincts as an actor are the only thing I have to offer and I wouldn't let them take that away from me. Ah... so it's very sweet. I don't want to put down Juilliard too much except to say it was not the right program for me at all and we both realized it.'

It wasn't the right program for Robin either, not that it mattered much in the longer term. However, he clearly harboured no ill will because in later years he funded other aspiring students to attend The Juilliard who would not otherwise have been able to do so. Jessica Chastain was one such beneficiary. 'I'm the first person in my family to go to college,' she told *Interview* magazine in 2011. 'We didn't have a lot of money, and Juilliard is a pretty expensive school. Robin Williams is a very generous Juilliard alumnus, and gives a scholarship every two years to a student, and it pays for everything, and I got it. I still haven't gotten to meet him.'

Understandably, in the wake of his death she was keen to pay tribute. 'Robin Williams changed my life,' she said.

'He was a great actor and a generous person. Through a scholarship, he made it possible for me to graduate college. His generous spirit will forever inspire me to support others as he supported me. He will forever be missed.'

In later years, of course, the various establishments where Williams studied were all exceedingly keen to ally themselves with a fine actor and comic genius, as he was. He even stayed in touch with some of them, including James Dunn at College of Marin, and his death came as a terrible shock to the institutions and individuals involved in his career, with many of them wishing to pay tribute to the master who had left them (and everyone else) behind.

'For the first time his eyes looked deep set and his face looked tired,' Dunn, who occasionally saw Williams over the years, told *MailOnline*, of the last occasion on which they met. 'He always had an impish charm about him for as long as I can remember but that vanished. There was always this aura around him. He always had women attention. You just couldn't not love him and that definitely rubbed off on the ladies. He was a womanizer, there's no doubt about that – and he always seemed to be able to deal with anything.' (It should be said that Dunn was speaking of the past, not Robin's marriage to his third wife, Susan Schneider, which had been extremely happy.)

'He was a sharp guy,' he continued. 'And even until recently Robin still seemed to be in good shape despite the major heart problems. There are some people who have demons but Robin wasn't that way, I never saw him as a dark person but some comics do have a dark side. I think it's hard to be funny and pull out the absurdities of life. He did a lot of drugs and then cleaned up on that. Then he got into alcohol and was in rehab a couple of times. When you look back on it you think, "Well, he lived life," he was like a moth to a flame – eventually he burnt out.'

It must be said that not everyone agrees with Dunn – many believe that Robin Williams had a very dark side indeed. Always there was an underlying sadness there, even in his most manic moments.

Naturally, The Juilliard was similarly affected by his death. Ironically or not, Robin Williams is among its most famous alumni, the boy considered too individual to train as an actor and yet turned out to be one of the finest actors of them all. It put out the following statement.

STATEMENT FROM THE JUILLIARD SCHOOL ON THE PASSING OF ROBIN WILLIAMS

The Juilliard community is deeply saddened by the death of our distinguished alumnus Robin Williams. Robin's genius for comedic improvisation, which quickly surfaced in his studies at Juilliard, was matched by his deep understanding of the actor's art and how to touch his audience in meaningful ways. He was a generous supporter of the School's drama students through the Robin Williams Scholarship, which supported the tuition cost of a drama student each year. As an artist, he brought together a unique mix of traditional actor training with a creative spirit that set new standards for performance in cinema, television and live theater. His caring ways and effervescent personality will be missed by all who were touched by this special person.

Joseph W. Polisi
President of The Juilliard School

CHAPTER FOUR

SEVENTIES
SENSATION

'Comedy is acting out optimism.'

ROBIN WILLIAMS

Post-Juilliard, Williams moved back to California, the place that was to become home for the rest of his life. Whatever his experiences had been to date – and his acting ambitions burned as strongly as ever – one thing was clear: he was blessed with a comic genius and he was going to put it to good use. In his own words though, it came about because his acting wasn't going so well: 'I left school and couldn't find acting work so I started going to clubs where you could do stand-up,' he said. 'I've always improvised and stand-up was a great relief. All of a sudden it was just me and the audience.' And didn't he put it to good effect?

Of course, Robin had some previous stand-up experience

but now it was time to make it his career. Already he had performed in San Francisco but now it was time to move on to the Los Angeles circuit, where he began to perform. And, as has been so very well documented since then, not least by Williams himself, he embarked on a journey of self-destruction, involving booze and drugs. He wasn't the only one… During this time he found out about 'drugs and happiness' he revealed, adding that he saw 'the best brains of my time turned to mud'.

The LA comedy club scene of the 1970s was to produce some of the finest talents in the American entertainment industry to this day. It is a mark of his genius that Williams stood out from the following, who all emerged round about the same time: David Letterman, Andy Kaufman, Jay Leno, Richard Lewis, Sam Kinison, Elayne Boosler, Tom Dreesen and George Miller. All were exceptional talents in their own right but Williams went on to eclipse everyone. Almost immediately he caused a sensation: 'He seemed to be omnipresent back then and was a topic of discussion wherever he went,' said the author Merrill Markoe. He was 'a comedy cyclone. In his act, he was id, ego and super-ego all at the same time.'

Much has been written about Robin's intense, utterly manic style of stand-up but in some ways it defies analysis, other than to say that the little boy who so desperately wanted the attention of his mother was not so eagerly begging for affection from the entire world. His performances went beyond energetic, beyond frenetic. At times they seemed dangerous, not because of the subject matter of the material (although it was often highly risqué) but because of what it said about the creator's own mental state. Vincent Canby, the American film critic who, like Williams, hailed from Chicago, once said the monologues were so intense that his 'creative process could reverse into a complete meltdown' – a very prescient observation, given what happened at the end was almost exactly that. Robin himself tried to explain it: the flow of ideas was never-ending, he said, because something was always happening in the world for him to react to. Free association kept the audience interested. And so on.

Williams cited many early influences on his act, including Jonathan Winters, Peter Sellers, Mike Nichols, Elaine May and Lenny Bruce. The reason he enjoyed their acts was that not only were they extremely funny, they were also highly intelligent. All were as erudite as he himself, although it is saying something that none of them, not even Sellers, who Robin most closely resembled as an actor, was anything like as intense.

He particularly admired the work of Jonathan Winters, the improvisational comic who appeared in the hit sci-fi comedy TV series *Mork & Mindy*, who was also a bundle of energy with a huge gift for mimicry. Williams' description of why he enjoyed him is a very apposite summary of his own work. 'That anything is possible, that anything is funny... He gave me the idea that it can be free-form, that you can go in and out of things pretty easily,' author, columnist and critic Gerald Nachman quotes him as saying. That was true enough and, to a certain extent, anyone could do stand-up… But to do it well? That required a very rare talent and one that it was increasingly obvious that Robin was cultivating in spades.

And he adored working with Winters. 'It was a joy,' he said in 2013 in an interview on *Reddit*. 'I believe I said in the Academy Awards it was like dancing with Fred Astaire but it was even better than that, because being around him, he would perform for anybody. There was no audience too small. I think I once saw him do a cat for a beagle. And I had the same experience watching *The Tonight Show* with my dad. Watching and laughing at Jonathan with my dad helped us become closer, very much so. My favorite Jonathan Winters' one-liner is "Have you ever undressed in front of a dog?"'

Williams was also a huge fan of Peter Sellers, having heard him on the BBC Home Service radio programme *The Goon Show*, which was groundbreaking in its time, and in an interview, he told presenter Michael Parkinson about Sellers' performance in the film *Dr. Strangelove*, 'It doesn't get any better than that.' Peter Cook and Dudley Moore, at the forefront of the early 1960s satire boom and another set of erudite and well-educated men, were also influences. Richard Pryor was yet another, although, like Robin, he was also to succumb to drink and drugs.

In fact, it is notable that, with the possible exceptions of Nichols and May, every single one of the artists Williams cited as early influences was not just extremely funny but very damaged indeed. Winters had had a couple of severe breakdowns and spent time in a psychiatric hospital. Peter Cook became an alcoholic. Dudley Moore struggled with depression. Peter Sellers was never capable of being himself: only happy when performing, he died of a heart attack aged just fifty-four, leaving behind a family full of tragedy and torment. Lenny Bruce was a drug addict, who died at the age of forty after taking an overdose. Richard Pryor, who also died relatively young (sixty-five) from a heart attack in December 2005, had drink and drug problems that, if anything, were worse than Robin's own. It was becoming more than mere coincidence. Indeed, the majority of the best comedians are damaged – they make people laugh to hide their own pain.

And so began a career that was both the best and the worst path that Williams could have chosen. Such was his energy and exuberance that it simply had to find an outlet somewhere and how better than in making people laugh? He talked about personal issues, he told the presenter Michael Parkinson, because it was 'cheaper than therapy' – a highly pertinent observation, not least because he himself was to end up in therapy throughout a great chunk of his life. And in some ways, this was true. If there were personal issues that could make him weep in his private life (and there were – Robin was far more easily moved to tears than anyone realised back then), it must have seemed a blessed relief to take those self-same issues and make people laugh.

But at the same time, it was a manic existence and not one designed to calm down a man already teetering on the edge. It was unstable: performances take place at night and the performer, having given it his all, ends on a high. Where to go from there? To another high, at that stage, this one chemically induced. Williams later revealed that he never drank or took drugs before a performance but he certainly did so afterwards and often performed with a hangover. He only once performed when high on cocaine, which, he said, made him paranoid; it was not a happy combination.

Then there was the fact that he was out on the road, constantly being made aware of other rising talents and surrounded by all manner of temptation that would prove hard to resist. 'It's a brutal field, man,' he is quoted as saying in Gerald Nachman's excellent book, *Seriously Funny: The Rebel Comedians of the 1950s and 1960s*. 'They burn out. It takes its toll. Plus, the lifestyle – partying, drinking, drugs. If you're on the road, it's even more brutal. You gotta come back down to mellow your ass out, and then performing takes you back up. They flame out because it comes and goes. Suddenly they're hot, and then somebody else is hot. Sometimes they get very bitter. Sometimes they just give up. Sometimes they have a revival thing and they come back again. Sometimes they snap. The pressure kicks in. You become obsessed and then you lose that focus that you need.'

Not everyone believed that Robin's problems were

worse than anyone else's though. It was, after all, the 1970s: practically everyone in show business was taking drugs. 'Anyone who grew up in that time had those experiences,' Chris Albrecht, CEO of Starz and a good friend of Robin's told *Variety*. 'Robin was not unique in that way. It was the 1970s.' That is certainly true but he also had a depressive streak, an addictive personality and a vulnerability that was not obvious when you saw him on stage or, indeed, for most people, in private. He had a self-destructiveness that would certainly not be helped by getting into drugs.

'Every night was different,' James Dulworth, who is now a manager at Dangerfield's Comedy Night Club in New York's Manhattan, revealed to *CBS News* after Williams' death. He had been a booker at the Comedy Store when Williams burst onto the scene. And he revealed that Robin's improvisation was actually a little more rehearsed than it seemed: 'He developed cards pretty much in his brain for any situation for every single night,' he said. 'He already had those ready for almost any situation. The owner of the Comedy Store was Mitzi Shore, Pauly Shore's mother,' he went on. 'I was working for her in the very beginning and she found [Williams] in San Francisco and brought him down [to Los Angeles].'

Others who saw him perform back then testify to a manic genius. 'He had the audience convulsing with laughter,' said Mark Breslin, who had hired Williams to perform in the club he then owned in Toronto. Now head of the Yuk Yuk's chain of comedy clubs, he was talking to

CBC News. 'He was doing characters and accents and crazy associations and word games. He turned the entire club into his stage. He walked on the tables and did comedy. He was completely amazing.'

The range of his subject matter startled people. One moment he would be quoting Shakespeare (quoting Shakespeare in the character of someone else, such as Jack Nicholson or Marlon Brando, was to remain a specialty and put to extremely good use in the 1989 movie *Dead Poets Society*); the next he'd be grabbing his crotch to make sure 'Mr Happy' was home. He veered all over the place, now pretending to be Elmer Fudd singing rock songs before branching out into a riff on the current political scene. It was impossible for the audience to get bored and equally for them to know what would happen next. 'Reality! What a concept!' he would cry but it was sometimes hard to know exactly what his grasp on reality was.

There was a mix of comedy and satire – material that would have been funny at any point and also something that was extremely topical, reflecting on current events. Was it exhausting? Williams was to continue his stand-up well into his television career, leaving the set to go out to entertain another audience but surely the mania and the energy must have had its dark side. Up on stage, the subject of adulation, he was basking in the glory of an audience that was hysterical with laughter but backstage afterwards it was like coming off a high. For someone with his personality it was, perhaps, inevitable that this would leave a hole that had to be filled somehow. And it wasn't difficult to see where that would be.

For even then it was apparent that he was a troubled soul. He was beginning to get into drink and drugs in a big way and the perceptive saw this would not end well. 'I'll never forget how sensitive he was,' said Dulworth. 'You could see how maybe he would become depressed. It probably wasn't easy to be him. He couldn't go out there and not be jovial and energetic. He probably needed some of those "boosters" to help maintain that fast-paced, energetic persona. He almost had to do the drugs to maintain that level of performance. It's almost like steroids with ball players.' But the fact remained that he was fast developing a drink and drugs problem that he would continue to do battle with for the rest of his life.

There were many other issues he had to deal with and the one that appeared to cause him the most personal hurt was that he stole other people's material. Most comedians will say that it is hard, at the very least, not to be aware of other people's material and to recycle it unintentionally but with Robin it went further than that. It finally came out in the public arena in 1989 when *GQ Magazine* wrote, 'His reputation for taking jokes and quickly making them his own in unequaled, dating back to his sudden emergence in the sitcom *Mork & Mindy*.' In fact, it pre-dated that. Some comedians not only accused him of blatant joke stealing but also refused to perform in front of him lest their material ended up coming out of his mouth.

'When he walks into a room,' the artistic coordinator of a prominent comedy club told *Rolling Stone* in 1991, 'a lot of comedians don't want to take the stage. I think Williams has got a huge cloud over his head, and I believe he's held at arm's length from the comedy community.' However, comedienne Whoopi Goldberg sprung to his defence. 'They made it sound as if Robin were taking their livelihood away,' she said. 'Comics do this all the time. Someone says a great line, and it stays with you, and you use it. We had "Make my day." Everybody was saying it, is that theft?'

Williams himself always said one of his most famous lines – 'Cocaine is God's way of telling you, you have too much money' – was given to him by a stranger. But it was a charge that rankled and did so for the rest of his life.

'I'm not gonna sit here and plead not guilty,' he told *Rolling Stone*. 'If you watch comedy eight hours a day, something will register, and it'll come out. And if it happened, I said, "I apologize. I'll pay you for this." But I wasn't going out of my way to go fucking grave robbing. 'Cause if you're on top, they're gonna look for your ass. Then I started getting tired of just paying, just being the chump,' he continued. 'I said, "Hey, wait a minute. It's not true." People were accusing me of stealing stuff that basically was from my own life. And then I went, "Wait, this is fucking nuts. I didn't take that. That's about my mother." A lot of comedy clubs are like Appalachian encounter groups,' he went on. 'Everybody's doing everybody else. You can go into a club and see fifteen different people, and they're all chewing each other apart. You say, "Hello, you prick. That's mine. I wrote Hello."'

So there was some professional jealousy going on but, eventually, so much so that he began insisting on standing outside a club before he went on to perform so that no one could ever accuse him of stealing their jokes. 'It's something I do now as a conscious effort, so no one can fucking accuse me. I'm not into necrophilia,' he told *Rolling Stone*. 'I don't need to go back and take "Oh, God, don't you just hate it about those medic-alert badges." Yeah, thanks. I'm taking that. That'll really work. And there [are] lots of people who took entire mannerisms from me. It's not something I can get mad about. It's flattery. It's great. When it happens the other way around, you're just supposed to smile.' It was true – he himself was to inspire a whole generation of comics. But this was to be a recurring theme and one that did not make life any easier.

However, on one front, things were looking up. In 1976 Robin was working in a bar in San Francisco when he met Valerie Velardi, who was a student at Mills College and working as a waitress to fund her way through her degree. The daughter of an Italian contractor, she came from New Haven, Connecticut, on the East Coast, and was the eldest of four. Her parents divorced when she was just twelve and Valerie assumed the role of mother after her real mother moved away. That might have contributed to her appeal for Robin. She was studying to become a dance teacher, having left it too late to become a dancer herself. 'A good, tough lady,' is how Robin described her to an interviewer and soon the two became an item. A month later they moved in together. She was to become Williams' first wife in 1978, and the pair enjoyed a very stormy relationship.

But Robin wasn't going to be working in a bar for long. The couple moved to Los Angeles, where he continued to work the comedy-club circuit, in 1977 performing at the Comedy Club, an appearance that changed his life. The television producer George Schlatter, a highly experienced and successful business pro, was in the audience. Born in Birmingham, Alabama, and raised in Webster Groves, Missouri, as a teenager Schlatter sang at the St Louis Municipal Opera, where his mother, a violinist, also performed. He went on to Pepperdine University in Los Angeles before joining MCA Records as an agent; after a few years he became the general manager of Ciro's Nightclub on the Sunset Strip.

It was while at Ciro's that he saw Dan Rowan and Dick Martin performing; coincidentally, he also started producing variety shows and specials for television. And it didn't take long for him to realise the two should mix. In 1967 he produced something that was meant to be a one-off special: *Rowan & Martin's Laugh-In* (the title was a reference to the various sit-ins and love-ins happening in fashionable society at the time). It was so successful that a regular series was commissioned, running from 1968 to 1973, and replacing *The Man From U.N.C.L.E.* on Monday nights at 8pm. Based on vaudeville, with a sprinkling of satire (the satire boom was then in full swing), there were gags, sketches and a great deal more. It was the first show to feature music videos on television and it was also, among much else, responsible for launching the career of actress Goldie Hawn.

The show had been one of the huge successes in television history and Schlatter was thinking about reviving it, so he was on the lookout for new talent. And boy, did he find it that night. 'He [Williams] extended the mic over the audience and said, "I'm fishing for assholes,"' Schlatter recalled. He was also looking to revive the *Laugh-In* show and so he booked Robin to appear on the NBC special *The Great American Laugh-Off* in late 1977. Schlatter was impressed, as so many were, by Williams' breadth of knowledge: 'He's one of the most well-educated comedians we've ever had,' Schlatter told *Variety*. 'Part of that came from the wealth of knowledge and expertise he developed at Juilliard.'

Robin was supposed to have a five-minute slot but this was extended to fifteen. And he was the unqualified success of the show: from the moment he first appeared, shaking hands with a bemused lady and squealing, 'She touched me like she knows me! I'm selling my clothes and going to Heaven!' it was evident a rarefied talent had arrived. The cast were required to open something that resembled stable doors, poke their heads out and introduce themselves: in Robin's case, the relevant door was actually in the floor but when he bobbed up to say his name, even in that instant alone, he exuded an extraordinary energy. Williams was also responsible for the one quote from the show to make it onto the IMDb website: 'Ladies and gentlemen, tonight I'm here to talk to you about the very serious problem of schizophrenia. – No he doesn't! – SHUT UP, LET HIM SPEAK!' He was the undisputed star of the evening, a major new talent now appearing on national TV.

Comedienne and TV host Joan Rivers met him during the making of the show but she was not quite so won over as everyone else. She felt that, in some ways, he was still auditioning – so determined to be noticed that he simply never stopped. 'You know how it is: You're struggling, you want to be noticed, and the only way is to be the funny boy,' she told *New York Magazine* in 1993. 'We took a picture together – and he never stopped mugging. You wanted to tie him down and say, "Stop."'

Everyone else, however, was totally won over. But Robin had been working up to this point for some years now. He had been honing his act in stand-up and his dedication at rehearsals was equal to his ability to improvise – far more preparation went into the act than most people realised. By now he was also developing a trademark look, one that he would stay with for a while: brightly coloured braces ('suspenders', as they were known in the States). No one could ever have described him as a snappy dresser but he knew the importance of presentation and creating an individual look that people could associate with him.

In the event, the show didn't exactly match the success of the original but it was obvious to everyone that a huge new talent had emerged on the scene. Schlatter signed him up to be part of his regular cast for the *Laugh-In* series of revivals he was planning. 'You didn't really need to bother writing for him,' said the humorist Merrill Markoe. 'When the camera was on, he blew through what he did and seized the show.' (Rowan & Martin themselves, incidentally, were not amused: they were not involved in the revival but owned the format to the show and so they went on to sue. They won $4.6 million in 1980.)

The speed of Williams' ascent was dizzying but it was to contribute to his problems too. It takes anyone some time to come to terms with being famous but, when it happens virtually overnight, the pressure can be almost too much to bear. Reality, for Robin, was changing very quickly – *too* quickly. Yet another reason to self-medicate began to manifest itself. Fame brings pressure and constant attention and he was having a hard time dealing with both.

There was also an appearance on *The Richard Pryor Show* but something much bigger was on the cards; something that meant he had to go to court to get out of his *Laugh-In* contract. It emerged that he was earning $1,500 an hour on *Laugh-In* and stood to earn $15,000 per episode if the new deal came off. In the event, he was successful in managing to get out of his contract, married Valerie and looked forward to a bright future. The wedding was a pretty major affair: the couple tied the knot at The Farms Country Club on 4 June

1978 in Wallingford, Connecticut, a country club where Valerie's father Leonard was a member. Both were certainly initially excited about the marriage, but the timing was not good because the sudden and dizzying change in Robin's status meant that he was about to experience a wild stage of his life. Through just one television appearance, he had made a huge impact and it had come to the attention of some very important people indeed.

One of the greatest comedians of the day was about to become a household name.

> 'We were talking briefly about cocaine… yeah.
> Anything that makes you paranoid and impotent,
> give me more of that!'
> ROBIN WILLIAMS

CHAPTER FIVE

NANU NANU

Mindy McConnell: *I can't believe you called all my friends!*
Mork: *I can't believe what they called you!*

Garry Marshall had a problem: the writer, director and producer had a long-running hit on his hands – *Happy Days* – about a happy family growing up in the 1950s and 1960s. It had started in 1974 and was to finish in 1984 but, halfway through the run, Marshall was trying to broaden its appeal. He turned to his son to ask what he wanted to watch and got a slightly unexpected reply.

'My 7-year-old son Scott was reluctant to watch *Laverne & Shirley* or *Happy Days* or any show I did,' he told *New York Magazine* in 1993. 'So I asked him, "What do you like?" He said, "I only like space." I told him, "I don't do space." "Well, you could do it." So I asked him, "How would you do space in *Happy Days*?" And he said, "It could be a dream." Now, this was the fourth year of the show, and we were trying to find worthy adversaries for Fonzie. So we wrote a guest role for Mork, the extraterrestrial. And my sister the casting agent brought Robin in from my sister Penny's acting class.'

As Marshall was later to observe, 'Williams was the only alien to audition for the role. He came into the room, Garry asked him to take a seat and Robin promptly put his head on the chair. It was immediately obvious that he was exactly right for the role: anarchic and a little bit crazy, you could easily believe he was actually an alien.'

'My job stopped being about remembering lines or moves, but to keep from laughing,' says Henry Winkler, the actor who played The Fonz, and who remembered it well. 'And yet Robin was so shy it was hard for him to speak. He did ask me, "After a day of this, how do you perform at the Comedy Store?" I told him, "After this, you really don't have the energy to perform at night."'

The Season Five episode 'My Favorite Orkan' (a reference to another TV series, *My Favorite Martian*) was broadcast in February 1978 and the viewers loved it. Admittedly, it was a little far-fetched: it involved an alien, Mork from the planet Ork, coming down to earth and trying to kidnap Richie Cunningham (Ron Howard) as a human specimen. The Fonz steps in and saves Richie and it is then revealed that Richie has been dreaming… to begin with, at least. When everyone involved absolutely loved it, the ending was changed so that, instead, it showed Mork wiping everyone's memories. Marshall was delighted: 'We said, "No, it's not a dream; it's real. It's another series!"'

It certainly was. And so *Mork & Mindy*, the show that would almost overnight turn Robin Williams into a household name, was born. The premise was that Mork (who has been grown in a test tube and drinks by using his finger) has been sent to Earth by Orson in a small, egg-shaped spaceship to observe humans. Orson wanted to get rid of him because humour is not permitted on Ork. Once down on Earth – he ends up in Boulder, Colorado, a place later to become the site of tributes to Robin – he dresses in a suit but puts it on backwards. He then encounters Mindy (Pam Dawber), who has just split from her boyfriend and takes him to be a priest, until he reveals who he actually is. She promises to keep his secret and to help him to study Earth. There is a flashback in which Mork tells her about when he came to Earth previously and The Fonz arranges for him to date Laverne De Fazio (from *Laverne & Shirley*, one of many crossovers between *Mork & Mindy* and other television series – Henry Winkler and Penny Marshall appeared).

Mork moves in with Mindy, much to her father Fred's chagrin (although her grandmother Cora, with whom she works in Fred's music store, likes him) but the local sheriff, Deputy Tilwick, who thinks Mork is unhinged, attempts to oust him. In the second episode, Mork agrees to leave but his plans are disrupted when he gets bezurb (drunk) on ginger beer and also reveals to Fred that he is actually an alien. The moving-out theme continues in the third episode when Mork has an attack of conscience after losing Mindy a date and, while looking for somewhere to stay, he encounters the eccentric Exidor, of which more below. In the next episode, Mindy tells Mork he must experience love to know what it is to be human – although this is clearly going to result in a 'will they?/won't they?' situation. Mork takes her at her word and falls in love with a mannequin named Dolly. By now it was clear why Robin was so right for the role: a child-like innocence was needed to pull this one off. But this is the episode in which Mork and Mindy kiss and the future is pretty clear.

The next episode, which sees a second kiss between the two of them, introduces the character of Susan (of which more below), who tries to make off with Mork in revenge for Mindy stealing her boyfriend in high school. But she doesn't succeed. Matters improve with Fred, who saves Mork's life after a newspaper reporter turns up looking for proof of alien life. Mork next pretends that he can predict the weather, prompting Mindy to tell him never to lie ('splinking'), after which he resuscitates the despicable landlord Arnold (of which more below.) The next episode sees Mork in jail with Exidor after falling for a sob story – somewhat uncomfortably for the modern viewer, Exidor worships O.J. Simpson. Mindy is briefly reunited with her ex-fiancé and Mork reduces himself to the age of three, using his Orkan age machine (this device was perfect for

Williams' talents and also enabled various other plot twists). Mork then rescues Mindy from an unwanted admirer, who is irate and with whom he must deal, following which he once again uses his age machine to become an older friend of Cora's, to whom he also reveals his true nature.

Next up, Mork learns the true nature of Christmas and teaches everyone else about it too, after he invites the unspeakable Susan to spend it with them as she has no one else (touches of Robin's future sentimental roles there), after which he mistakes a Russian immigrant for being an alien. An irritating new neighbour, Franklin, moves in, after which Mork performs a wedding ceremony for two friends. Exidor is back, planning to become Emperor of Earth, and lets the couple use his summer home but chaos ensues. Mork is threatened with a transfer, Sally returns with a newborn son, who Mork loves so much that he buys a baby of his own, and then, in an episode that won considerable acclaim, Mork shuts his emotions down after a nightmare. Mindy kisses him to release those emotions, which Mork cannot control. Again, it was the perfect comedic vehicle for Williams.

Mindy goes away and Mork and Mr Bickley visit a singles bar: there they meet ladies who turn out to be thieves. Mr Bickley then becomes a thief too and steals Mork's age machine, changing his age from a baby to middle age. Mork tries to find a job but his 'birthday' causes a potentially fatal condition (he must recharge himself with an egg-like 'gleek') and he then loses Mindy a job. When he finds out, he tells Orson that he wishes he'd never come to Earth but Orson shows him what would have happened had he not done so: Mindy would have married gambling addict Cliff, Fred would have gone off on his travels and had a short-term relationship, Cora would have been living with Mindy and the music shop would have been sold. The episode was called 'It's A Wonderful Mork', in reference to the heartwarming 1946 Christmas fantasy film *It's A Wonderful Life*. The final episode of the season – the twenty-fifth – has Exidor back as a reincarnation of Julius Caesar and Mork makes a pet of a caterpillar called Bob. And so the series drew to a close.

There could scarcely have been a finer vehicle for Williams' talents. He improvised a great deal of his role and became extremely famous almost overnight. Indeed, he improvised so much that there would be gaps in the script, left there to allow him to create his own monologue. It was difficult for his co-star Pam Dawber, simply because she had to stop herself from laughing as she watched. The audience certainly found the whole thing totally hilarious: the show was a massive hit, with 60 million viewers regularly tuning in. Paramount hastily signed Robin up to a five-year $3 million contract. Williams came from a wealthy background anyway but, for the first time, it looked as if he would now be seriously rich.

The *Mork & Mindy* TV series soon entered popular culture. People began greeting each other with the phrase 'Nanu nanu', accompanied by a Mr Spock-esque Vulcan salute. The word 'shazbot', an Orkan profanity, entered the language, as did 'KO', Mork's version of OK. Eventually, the series overtook *Happy Days* in the ratings. Those were heady times. Robin and Valerie moved to a canyon home and Robin bought a silver BMW; they started to have a few animals. But he was also beginning to party hard and after a day on set he was either out socialising or doing stand-up, which is not a recipe for domestic bliss. And it didn't help that Valerie wasn't enjoying the partying, with the unfortunate result that Robin was often out on his own. He still wore his Hawaiian shirts and baggy trousers but he'd had to give up the multi-coloured braces because they made him too recognisable. Fame was beginning to encroach on his life. He was linked to the model Molly Madden; Valerie was seen on her own in Italy. On the plus side, he also started doing charity work for, among others, the Human Dolphin Foundation: something he would continue for the rest of his life.

Things changed in the show's second season, however, and arguably suffered as a result. The emphasis moved from Mork's attempts to understand Earth to his relationship with Mindy and, in an attempt to address social issues rather than just delight in the comedy, a younger audience was targeted, with Fred and Cora leaving their regular roles, although they did return in later episodes. Various new characters were introduced. Somewhat unwisely, the show was shifted into a number of different time slots and the audience began falling away.

'That was kind of depressing at first because I took it on myself personally, thinking, "Oh, God! I'm not funny anymore",' Williams told *New York Magazine* in a 1981 interview. 'At last I realized that it was a combination of other things. They were screwing around with the schedule, changing the time slot every other night. And parents got angry when we started doing all those sexploitation shows – written specifically to get little girls running around in tight outfits and me dressing in drag. That lost a lot of people who used to watch with their kids. Also, some people thought we were heavy-handed talking about things like euthanasia; we had that one show about the robot being unplugged.' It was certainly a far cry from the merry mayhem at the start.

There were also increasing rumours about Robin's personal life, with his name now openly linked to a selection of other women. He was forced to make a conscious effort to calm down. 'It's not the work but the social life that drained me,' he told *People Magazine* in 1979. 'I was bordering on exhaustion. I got so frenetic I scared myself. There was no time to recover, no time to go home and say, "Screw you" to a wall. I was starting to go through the roof. You have to say "No" or else you go slowly bozo.'

Meanwhile, Valerie was making more of an effort too: she had accepted that she was now married to a famous actor and attempted to play the game, attending industry events with him and being an industry wife, as well as working, on an ad hoc basis, as a dance teacher.

But the show was flailing. There were more attempts to jig up the ratings and, in the fourth season, Mork and

Mindy were married. Mork laid an egg and they had a child – Mearth, played by Jonathan Winters (it was explained that Orkans age backwards). But the magic had gone and, in 1982, the show was duly cancelled. In total, ninety-one episodes had been filmed. The experience taught Williams a lesson he never forgot: namely, don't be complacent. 'I found out the show was cancelled by reading it in *Variety*,' he told *People* in a 2009 interview. 'In Hollywood that's like reading your own obituary: "You're dead, good luck!"' For a man given to such personal insecurity, it was all a little unfortunate.

The series spawned a great many much-loved characters, apart from Mork and Mindy themselves. Tetchy old Fred (Conrad Janis) and freethinking Cora (Elizabeth Kerr) both had big fan bases and, in retrospect, it was a huge mistake to downgrade their characters. Franklin Delano Bickley (Tom Poston) was a next-door neighbour; Mearth (Jonathan Winters) their giant, elderly child. Siblings Remo and Jean Davinci (Jay Thomas and Gina Hecht) were co-owners of The New York Delicatessen. Nelson Flavor (Jim Staahl) was Mindy's conservative, ambitious cousin. Then there was the long-suffering Orson (voiced by Ralph James), Mork's superior.

There were other recurring characters with their own roles on the show. Susan Taylor (Morgan Fairchild) is a snooty friend of Mindy's from high school. Exidor (Robert Donner) is a prophet who recognises Mork for what he is and the leader of a cult that no one else can see. Mr Sternhagen (Foster Brooks) becomes Mindy's boss at the local TV station; Todd Norman Taylor (TNT) (Bill Kirchenbauer) is a womanising jock who teaches Mork how to drive. Eugene (Jeffrey Jacquet) is a ten-year-old boy who befriends Mork in the first series; Billy (Corey Feldman) is a daycare-centre child. The somewhat unfortunately named (to a British audience at least!) Arnold Wanker (Logan Ramsey) is the landlord of Fred's music store.

Oddly, for something that started out as such a frothy piece of fun, *Mork & Mindy* hinted at various elements that were to affect Williams' life. He was an extremely talented actor, and recognised as such by even the most churlish reviewers, but what he excelled at above and beyond anything else was comedy, especially improvisational comedy. However, one criticism often levelled at him was that he was at times just too sentimental and he neglected his real gift for something that could be a little cloying. And that is exactly what happened to *Mork & Mindy*: the series started out as wildly comedic but ended up being a programme that tried to comment on the issues of the day. This didn't work and audiences didn't like it. And, although it would be easy to lay the blame at the door of the producers, Robin was also himself involved in the decision-making process.

This was brought home in an episode ('Mork Meets Robin Williams') from 1981 that was frankly self-indulgent. Mindy goes out and buys an album by the comic Robin Williams. On returning home she realises he is the spitting image of Mork. Robin himself then enters and debates the nature of massive celebrity and, when Mork tunes in to Orson, he tells him, 'Being a star is a twenty-four hour job and you can't leave your face at the office... some of them can't take it.' He then lists the names of some of those who were destroyed by the pressures of fame: Elvis Presley, Marilyn Monroe, Jimi Hendrix, John Lennon... Given that this episode aired just two months after Lennon's death, the message was loud and clear: fame can be fatal. It was admittedly an eerie presentiment of Williams' own fate, to say nothing of an indication of his state of mind, but it was having his cake and eating it. Nor was it funny and it was not what the audience wanted.

It did, however, give some indication of what was happening behind the scenes. In a few short years Williams had gone from virtual unknown to being one of the most famous men in the world and this was bound to take its toll. Even the most balanced and stable of beings would have found it difficult to deal with and he was neither of those things. In addition, a part of him resented that he was now so closely associated with his alien creation: when he went out to perform live at nightclubs, which he still very much did (often after a day's filming), the audience would shout, 'Do Mork!' But Robin didn't want to do Mork.

Always prone to self-destruction, now the crisis really began. Along with his friend and fellow comedian John Belushi, Williams was getting heavily into drugs and alcohol and this was taking its toll on everything in his life. Now that he was famous and increasingly rich, women were beginning to throw themselves at him. Frequently drunk and/or high, he wasn't always turning them down. Of course, this was bound to have a detrimental effect on his marriage and it did. Matters were becoming extremely fraught behind the scenes.

At first Valerie seemed able to cope. She wanted to fight for her man. 'Look, I'm a product of Goddard College,' she told *Rolling Stone* in 1982 in an extremely revealing interview that hinted at much greater turmoil in the background. 'Are you familiar with it? And one thing it's taught me is that you can guide people; you can make yourself interesting enough and important enough in your lover's life so that he'll always come back to you if you just keep growing along with it. If you just be part of their rhythm and give them a lot of freedom and be part of their growth instead of pulling them back from what is titillating and exciting. Let's face it, Robin is a stimulus junkie.'

He certainly was, far more so than anyone yet realised. Now not only was the situation reaching a point where it was unsustainable, it was also increasingly difficult to live with. But Valerie was putting a brave face on it – for now. Asked about other women, she replied, 'That means no, in a situation like that – it's a rough one, because I could be misquoted horribly. See, the thing is, it was never any one woman. It was lots of women, and I'm not sure he had something intimately to do with them all. Most of it was just hanging out. He loves women and he likes hanging out with women. I have this letter from a woman who

Robin was seen around town with. They were supposed to be having a hot, uh, affair, and I got to know her and she was lovely. They just wanted to hang out. I can't stop him from having dinner with a woman he likes. That's none of my business, just like I wouldn't like him to stop me from hanging out with anyone I wanted to go out with. If he can't have women friends and I can't have men friends, if you have to keep assuming the worst every time someone finds someone else to enrich their lives in some way, what kind of a world is this?'

What about jealousy? 'I get jealous. I'd only get jealous if I felt someone were taking my place,' she went on. 'And it's always been very clear that we've got it. It's us. It doesn't sit right, but under extraordinary circumstances, which we are under, if you don't make the necessary adjustments, then you can lose precious things. That's not to say that gives us the license to go off and screw everything that's around. It's just the freedom to at least feel like we're free individuals as opposed to being married and locked in and you can't go out tonight because I know so and so is there and she's hot and pretty and I'm afraid you're gonna get involved with her. He's never gonna get involved with anyone without me knowing about it. And the other way doesn't work. You can't hold somebody in. They resent you, hate you, you become boring and unattractive. If I had jumped the gun and divorced him, I would have lost the most precious thing in my life and it would have curtailed our experience together, which is a lot richer than anything he can get off the street.'

Valerie's resilience was extremely admirable but it was never going to work. The relationship was becoming increasingly stormy: Robin was essentially doing what he wanted and provoking her so badly that she would storm out, take herself off for a few days' hiking, sometimes go on holiday and only come back when she had calmed down. Her attitude at that stage was that, while Robin might have been behaving badly, the other women didn't mean anything to him. She was his wife, after all. But while this was true, it was increasingly difficult to ignore the fact that success had turned her husband into a drug-abusing womaniser. Matters were, in fact, going to get even messier but she was intent on keeping things going for now.

And who can blame her? In some respects, life had improved for her too: being married to a big star might entail its own pressures but, at the same time, the couple were beginning to experience a very decent standard of living indeed. It wasn't just the best tables at the best restaurants; everyone wanted to meet Robin these days. He was talked about everywhere and that sort of fame opened the kind of doors that are closed to most of us. And then again, of course, when he was on form, Robin was stunningly good company. Valerie, understandably, wanted the relationship to work out.

By now Robin had bought a house in Topanga Canyon and another car: an old Land Rover – 'I can't deal with new cars. I like a car that's like me – you never know what's going to happen next.' He was certainly not that interested in material things for their own sake, although by now the money was coming in fast.

What he did want though was a Hollywood career and, in 1980, he made his proper film debut in what was widely considered to be a disappointment: *Popeye*, with Shelley Duvall co-starring as Olive Oyl. (He had also appeared in a 1977 film, *Can I Do It 'Till I Need Glasses*. Mercifully, this had been forgotten and is almost never mentioned in the Williams' oeuvre. It sank like a trace and deservedly so.) There had been high hopes resting on this, his latest production, not least because the director was Robert Altman and the producer Robert Evans (the original leads had been scheduled to be Dustin Hoffman and Lily Tomlin), but the musical comedy was a critical flop (although not a commercial one, comfortably raking in twice its $30 million budget at the box office).

One problem was the plot, which was confusing and all over the place. Not all the critics hated it but some certainly did. 'E.C. Segar's beloved sailorman boards a sinking ship with this astonishingly boring musical,' wrote respected critic Leonard Maltin in his movie guide. 'A game cast does its best with an unfunny script, cluttered staging and some alleged songs. Tune into a few hours' worth of Max Fleischer cartoons instead; you'll be much better off.' The only aspect of the movie to garner praise was Harry Nilsson's soundtrack, which was well received. But for the rest of it, most people thought it was a bit of a mess.

It was a disappointing debut for someone of whom so

much was now expected but Robin took it on the chin. He had several more seasons of *Mork & Mindy* to go and producers and directors were still queuing up to work with him. While some flops have brought film careers to a premature end, this was certainly not the case here. Williams was riding higher and higher on a wave of adulation as Hollywood continued to savour the talented newcomer and only his inner circle knew that he was paying a terrible price. His drug taking was increasingly out of control and his marriage still suffered because, intoxicated by everything coming his way, he behaved like a child let loose in a candy store when it came to women. Valerie could only look on and despair.

It wasn't just the wealth and fame that made him attractive either. Robin genuinely liked women and was a terrible flirt. On top of that, his wit and vivacity were enormously attractive in themselves, let alone in someone who was fast becoming such a huge star. Valerie persevered and the marriage was to last for a while yet but it was becoming increasingly difficult for the couple to maintain a happy façade. There were rows and unhappiness and, although Valerie sometimes thought that Robin had turned a corner, the truth was that he hadn't. He was fast becoming known as a drug-taking womaniser and it would take a tragedy to force him to confront the fact that his demons were now spiraling out of control.

'I like my wine like my women — ready to pass out!'
ROBIN WILLIAMS

CHAPTER SIX

THE WORLD ACCORDING TO ROBIN

*'You know, everybody dies. My parents died. Your father
died. Everybody dies. I'm going to die too. So will you.
The thing is, to have a life before we die. It can be a real
adventure having a life.'*

JENNY FIELDS (GLENN CLOSE), *THE WORLD
ACCORDING TO GARP* (1982)

By the early 1980s Williams was certain about what he
wanted to do: to go into mainstream acting. This had,
after all, been the initial intention: he had trained at The
Juilliard as an actor, not a stand-up comic and, if they
hadn't seen his potential there, the fault was with them.
And while *Popeye* had been a disappointment, there were
plenty more projects in the pipeline. But what he went
for next startled everyone.

The World According To Garp (1982) was John Irving's fourth novel, a bestseller and winner of the National Book Award for Fiction. It was to be turned into a film, coincidentally also starring John Lithgow in a leading role. (Lithgow later starred in the TV series *3rd Rock From The Sun* [1996–2001], another alien in a suburban-setting comedy, which owed a great deal to *Mork & Mindy*.) It started with Jenny Fields (Glenn Close, at that point not yet very famous – this was her screen debut), a nurse in the Second World War who impregnates herself via a dying soldier known only as Garp. She duly gives birth to a son.

Garp grows up to become a successful writer, married to Helen Holm (Mary Beth Hurt), with whom he has two children, Duncan and Walt, while Jenny turns into something of a feminist icon. Helen becomes involved with one of her students, something Garp finds out about, and he crashes into his wife's lover's car as she performs a sex act on him. Walt is killed in the crash and Duncan hurt in one eye. Despite this, the couple somehow reconcile and go on to have another child, Jenny.

The original Jenny is now running a centre for transsexuals, and it is on a visit to the centre that Garp hears about Ellen James, a girl who was gang-raped and then had her tongue cut out so that she could not identify her attackers. Some of the women at Jenny's centre are 'Ellen Jamesians', women who voluntarily cut out their own tongues in a show of solidarity. Garp is horrified by the practice and learns that the Jamesians have received a letter from Ellen James herself begging them to stop this practice but they have voted to refuse.

Jenny is the subject of death threats and so, too, after he writes a book about Ellen James, is Garp. Jenny is shot and killed by an anti-feminist fanatic. The women at the centre hold a memorial for her but forbid all men from attending. Dressed as a woman, Garp is secreted into the memorial but his identity becomes known and he is in danger from the women, one of whom leads him out and turns out to be Ellen James. However, he, too, is eventually shot and, as he is taken away in an air ambulance, he has one last memory of his mother tossing him into the air as a child.

Mork & Mindy it was not, nor indeed *Popeye*. This was a solid, meaty dramatic role that needed an actor of some skill and ability to take it on and, given that Williams was known almost entirely for the role of Mork and his stand-up comedy, the world of show business was astounded when news of the casting leaked out.

'A lot of people thought I was crazy to cast Robin,' director George Roy Hill (*Butch Cassidy & The Sundance Kid/The Sting*) told *New York Magazine* in an interview before the film was released. 'But you make these decisions instinctively. I'd seen him as Popeye and didn't understand a word he said. I'd seen him once as Mork and didn't understand him either. I thought he was just a stand-up comic. But on meeting him, I felt he had a sense of decency that was important. Garp is an abrasive man, but his underlying decency is a key part of the character, and I felt Robin was the sort of actor who could provide that. I hope I'm right.'

In fact, he turned out to be one of the first in Hollywood to see that Robin Williams was far more than the comic he had previously been regarded as. A superbly gifted actor, he had the depth and emotional intelligence to take on a more serious role. *The World According To Garp* was billed as a comedy drama, although it dealt with extremely serious issues and was, therefore, bound to be controversial.

'Robin is an extraordinary talent,' George Roy Hill said. 'He's an actor, a real actor, not just a comedian who is put into a role requiring acting. He can go the whole distance if he puts his mind to it. I'd say he's one of the brightest men I've ever met. He's got a tremendous mind, and while he's not an intellectual, he could qualify as one eventually. He's quick, instinctive, funny, and warm, and one of the few comedians I've ever met who, while "on" a lot of the time, is not offensively "on." Garp's not a comic character. He's a very serious character, but there is comedy, most of it based on reality. In the film, Robin has to go from 18 years old to 34. In fact, he's 29, but he's always had an old face. I've looked at pictures of him at 18 or 19, and he looks older, so he's believable when he has to play that age.'

All the same, it was to prove a learning experience. Williams had to learn how to control himself: his stand-up comedy depended on a rapid-fire delivery, as did his portrayal of the alien Mork – indeed, his ability to talk so quickly was one of the many things that made him right for the part. George Roy Hill acknowledged this. 'Robin had a habit we had to overcome,' he said. 'He's inclined to too fast delivery – it took me a long time to slow him down to a playing speed, since his mind works so fast. I think I've got him slowed down enough, although maybe it's just that I'm getting used to him.'

For Robin, too, it was quite an experience and not just in learning how to slow his delivery down. This was a world away from the kind of material he was used to: a demanding dramatic role that was not particularly easy to pull off. 'The main problem is in making all the different ages fit together,' he disclosed in 1981 to *New York Magazine*. 'I have to make all those phases of life and the different relationships believable. I've had to go really deep inside myself, to examine painful and wonderful things. There are lively scenes dealing with children; there's a lot of death and dealing with loss. Scenes with my wife in the film are very personal, no pretense at all. I have to be very direct, very open.'

He also betrayed a real insecurity; the first public hint of a much more vulnerable personality than had ever been seen before. At that stage in his life, Williams was still very much seen as a clown: a brilliantly talented one, of course, but a clown nonetheless. No one really knew about the depths of his depression, the solitary side, the aching void within that drink and drugs and comedy were all being used to kill – no one in public, at any rate. To those close to Robin, it was obvious that he was nothing like as straightforward as he sometimes seemed.

'I haven't gone to see the rushes, because I'm afraid they would jar me,' he admitted. 'I don't think I'll get a view of myself until the final cut. It's like drowning, like running for your life. I have no perspective. It's not like comedy or all-out farce, where I know my instincts. It's all unknown territory. It's like being in combat. I finished one day of shooting and thought, "God, I died." Even though it was only a single scene, I had this bizarre feeling, and I wept for a couple of hours after it. When I finally see the film, I'll look back and say, "I did that." I'll be proud. I feel proud now, but I just can't say it yet because it's not over. It's a gamble. It's scary, really bizarre, because every time you do something totally new, you suddenly think, "Oh, no. Now it's over. From now on I'll be selling the *National Enquirer* door to door."'

Of course, many actors have that terrible sense of insecurity: that one day they will be found out and will have to return to the life they led before. But in Robin's case, this was accentuated by the fact that it had all happened so fast. It almost didn't matter that *Mork & Mindy* was, by now, fast losing ratings and would shortly be coming to an end. He had made the leap into the big time but, in common with so many others, he couldn't see the strength of his own position. In the midst of the maelstrom that was now his life, he couldn't see clearly that he was now so sought after that a successful career was pretty much assured from then on.

'I'm amazed and in shock sometimes,' he confessed when asked about his fame by *New York Magazine*. 'Sometimes I feel like I could be back to ground zero again. I go through these phases of getting terrified. I can't really cope with them because they're debilitating. I have to try new things – like *Garp* – push myself out. You know – the next chance. Because my greatest fear is of becoming mediocre, just falling back into the old rut and turning out the same old stuff without really finding anything new. That's also true for life – just trying not to get stuck, this fear of falling back, sinking back into myself.'

But at least his relationship with Valerie was currently on an even keel. For Robin wasn't just slowing his delivery, he was slowing the manic pace of his life as well and was appreciating his wife and his marriage. After all, Valerie had known him before he was famous and one major issue for many of the rich and famous is whether their friends and partners like them because of their status or who they really are. That was not an issue: having married Robin when he was a complete unknown, Valerie was one of the few people with whom he could really be himself.

'She should really go back and teach,' he told *New York Magazine*. 'She has a very strong pride about not wanting to be known as Mrs. Robin Williams.

'In the beginning there were no managers, no press people, just the two of us. She was important just being there, going to clubs with me, hanging out with me. Now we've gone beyond that into another phase. It's sheer emotional.

ROBIN WILLIAMS

It's nice to come home to somebody who knows you. I can sit down and not say anything. Sometimes I pass out. The other day I was wrestling for thirteen hours. I couldn't say anything when I got back. I don't have to entertain or do anything. She understands. I love her so much. I look at her sometimes and feel very peaceful. We've been through crazy things, the wild and wooly times. Now it's like, "Look – land!" *Garp* has kicked off something in me. The really simple things please me now. I like taking long walks, being outside, just doing things with friends more than I did before. It's wonderful. Before, I had to go out and party, perform, and always be "on." Now I'm content to listen and sit back.'

For now, at least… there was trauma yet to come.

The World According To Garp was released in July 1982 and Williams was a revelation, to the critics at least. They did not necessarily award the film entirely positive reviews, not least because many appeared to like neither the odd story nor the book upon which it was based, but they were impressed by what they had seen.

'Robin Williams displays the acting chops that would win him an Oscar,' said Alex Sandell of *Juicy Cerebellum*. 'Good effort, sometimes nearly great,' declared Ken Hanke in the *Mountain Xpress*.

'Steve Tesich adapted *The World According to Garp* for the screen, and George Roy Hill directed,' wrote Frederic and Mary Ann Brussart in *Spirituality and Practice*. 'Tesich's sterling humanism and Hill's healthy respect for life's seriocomic dimensions made this film one of the best movies of 1982. The performances are all top-drawer. The storyline – true to the spirit of the novel – compels us to consider the ambiguities of love, death, sex, and violence that characterize modern life.'

'Garp just doesn't get it, and for good reason. Despite his odd conception and upbringing, he's the eternal Everyman,' wrote James Kendrick of Q *Network Film Desk*. 'He just wants to have a good family, and be remembered for something. His life of suburban normalcy pales in comparison to his mother's feminist resort, populated with tongueless women and sexually altered football players like Roberta Muldoon (John Lithgow). Robin Williams may seem like an odd choice to play such a normal guy, but he actually works well in the role. He's good at conveying his utter bewilderment at the strange goings-on around him, while Jenny just stands back and smiles, never once thinking that any of this is odd.'

Meanwhile, *Variety* was complimentary about the film, though not entirely sure about Robin. 'Garp grows up in a placid academic environment, and the grown man in the person of Robin Williams appears after only 25 minutes,' it wrote. 'He meets and marries Mary Beth Hurt, raises his family, fitfully pursues his writing while she teaches, has skirmishes with the feminists at his mother's mansion, and all the while tries to avoid the "undertoad", the unseen, pervasive threat which lurks everywhere and strikes without warning. Physically, Williams is fine, but much of the performance is hit-and-miss. Otherwise, casting is superior. Hurt is excellent as Garp's wife. Glenn Close proves a perfect choice as Jenny Fields, a woman of almost ethereal simplicity. Best of all, perhaps, is John Lithgow as Roberta Muldoon, a former football player, now a transsexual.'

Time Out also wasn't convinced. 'Williams is cuddly enough as the man whose talents for nurturing a family are constantly undermined by a malign fate, and there is a performance of some dignity from Lithgow as a six-and-a-half-foot ex-pro footballer transsexual,' it said. 'But it's the kind of movie which is brave – or stupid – enough to ask the meaning of life without having enough arse in its breeches to warrant a reply.'

Some noted the development in Robin's career from comic to actor. 'Mr. Williams is at his most affecting with the children; he makes a fond, playful father, a man perfectly at home in a suit of make believe armor made of welcome mats and garbage-can lids,' wrote Janet Maslin in *The New York Times*. 'Mr. Williams's role is a very demanding one, calling on him to age from a teenager to a family man, a process he has trouble with. His performance is engaging but erratic, more effective in the clownier, busier scenes than in those that ask him to recite lines or stand still. Mr. Williams is much less compelling at rest than he is when free to represent Garp through action. When the role doesn't call for movement of some kind, he falters.'

And some just couldn't get on with the film. 'What are

we to think of these people and the events in their lives?' asked the rather more skeptical Roger Ebert in the *Chicago Sun-Times*. 'I thought the acting was unconventional and absorbing (especially by Williams, by Glenn Close as his mother, and by John Lithgow as a transsexual). I thought the visualization of the events, by director George Roy Hill, was fresh and consistently interesting. But when the movie was over, my immediate response was not at all what it should have been. All I could find to ask myself was: What the hell was that all about?'

Pauline Kael was none too happy either: 'There's no feeling of truth in either the book or the movie,' she declared, and the 'generally faithful adaptation seems no more (and no less) than a castration fantasy.'

Whatever people thought about it, however, it had made the point that Robin Williams could act. Some, including the film critic Roger Ebert, were to maintain the view that he was essentially a comedian rather than an actor but, from now on, it was clear that his talents ran far deeper than anyone had realised up until then. And it was good timing too: *Mork & Mindy* had just come to a close and now it was time to get on with life's next act.

But three months before the movie came out something happened that was to have a profound effect on Williams' life. In March 1982, aged just thirty-three, his close friend and fellow actor and comic John Belushi died of a drug overdose, after consuming a speedball (a mixture of cocaine and heroin). He was found dead in his room at the Chateau Marmont on Sunset Boulevard. In the early hours on the day of his death he was visited both by Williams and fellow actor Robert De Niro. It was a terrible shock for all concerned.

Like Williams, Belushi was one of Hollywood's rising stars. He, too, had made his name on television – in his case *Saturday Night Live* – and, like Williams, he was a staggeringly talented comic performer, now probably best remembered for his role in *The Blues Brothers* (1980), with his great friend Dan Aykroyd, who penned the role of Dr. Peter Venkman in *Ghostbusters* (1984) with him in mind (the part later went to Bill Murray). Like Williams, his ascent was meteoric and he, too, was beginning to learn what a shark pool Hollywood can be. The day before his death, Paramount Pictures had been pressurising him to appear in *National Lampoon's The Joy Of Sex* (1984), something Aykroyd very much advised against, saying they were just using Belushi's involvement to get the picture made: 'Oh, don't do that piece, are you kidding me?' he told his friend. 'Get out, get away! Come home, it's the spring, something will happen over the summer or fall.' That something would almost certainly have been *Ghostbusters* but it was not to be.

Despite this encouragement, Belushi agreed to do the film. Perhaps it was his innate disgust at the project or maybe it was just that his drug use was now hopelessly out of control but he spent his last night with another notorious drug user, Catherine Evelyn Smith, a former back-up singer for The Band, among others, veering between The Roxy theatre and the Chateau Marmont, with Smith repeatedly injecting him with heroin. The next morning he was found dead in his bed. Smith was later arrested and charged with first-degree murder; she eventually plea bargained this down to manslaughter and served eighteen months' imprisonment.

Williams had been there earlier, snorting several lines of coke, but it seemed he was repulsed by Smith, whom he found 'creepy'. Somewhat unfortunately, it has been said that he left that night with the words, 'If you ever get up again, call me.' Though meant to be a throwaway line, it was frighteningly prescient. Although he was in no way to blame, Robin was to suffer enormous guilt in the wake of that night, although, in truth, by that stage it was unlikely that anyone could have saved John. His friend and co-performer Penny Marshall (who directed Robin in *Awakenings*, 1990) revealed decades later that John was absolutely incapable of resisting any kind of temptation, with inevitable and sad results. 'I swear, you'd walk down the street with him, and people would hand him drugs. And then he'd do all of them – be the kind of character he played in sketches or *Animal House*,' she told *The Hollywood Reporter* over thirty years after his death. 'I love him, and I miss him, and I wish he hadn't gotten in with the people he was around. But in the '70s and '80s, people were crazy.'

John Belushi's early death was a terrible shock to Hollywood and the wider world. His widow, Judy, who had been his childhood sweetheart, was beside herself. Close associates knew Belushi to be an addict but, even so, he had such a promising future ahead of him that no one could quite believe what had happened.

'What can I say? John was excessively talented, and I guess you could say he sort of lived life "excessively,"' said the music producer Bruce Robb, who had worked with him in the past and was also a close associate of Dan Aykroyd. 'I think what happened to John had a sobering effect on a lot of people, me included.'

And it had a shattering effect on Robin, for John had been a good friend. He had seen him only hours before he died and there were too many parallels between the two of them not to be concerned that the same thing might happen to him. Then again, it must be said that his own drug taking was not on a level with John's. 'It was a strange thing because my managers sent me to this doctor because they said I had this cocaine problem,' he told the *Los Angeles Times* in 1991. 'He said, "How much do you do?" And I said, "A gram every couple of days," and he said, "You don't have a problem." That was before they'd started to acknowledge it was psychologically addicting. And then at a certain point you realize, maybe it is. Physically I'm not craving it, but mentally I'm really thinking it might be a good idea.'

He was certainly doing enough to realise his habit was in danger of spiralling out of control and he was drinking heavily too. It was one of those pivotal moments in a person's life when things can go either way. Like Belushi, Williams was a young man who had burst onto the scene and had a huge future ahead of him. He could choose to embrace that future or he could give in to the dark side, with all the risks that entailed.

There were other reasons for going sober as well. Robin and Valerie were giving their marriage another go, so much so that, a few months after John's death, Valerie became pregnant with Robin's first child. Robin might have been wild and reckless at that stage but he was not foolish, and to introduce a baby into the kind of lifestyle he was experiencing was simply not on. He knew he had to stop and so he did. At that stage, he did not go into rehab, as he was to do in later life but, through sheer willpower, he gave everything up, going cold turkey. For decades afterwards he was clean.

'The Belushi tragedy was frightening,' he told *People* many years later. 'His death scared a whole group of show business people. It caused a big exodus from drugs. And for me, there was the baby coming. I knew I couldn't be a father and live that sort of life.'

It seemed a new chapter was opening and, to a certain extent, it was. Robin was just at the start of an extraordinarily successful film career, he had cleaned up his act and he and Valerie had a baby on the way. But he was never quite able to rid himself of his demons. Although his marriage was back on track, he would soon find himself immersed in an affair that resulted in a spectacularly embarrassing court case, making headlines for all the wrong reasons and, despite the fact that he and Valerie worked at it, their marriage was not to last.

In one of life's great ironies, Robin Williams, who brought so much joy and laughter to those around him and who was to become such a great entertainer, was never able to make peace with himself.

'Spring is nature's way of saying, "Let's party!"'
ROBIN WILLIAMS

CHAPTER SEVEN

TROUBLED TIMES

'I went to rehab in wine country,
just to keep my options open.'
ROBIN WILLIAMS

London, England. It was the early 1980s and one of
Hollywood's hottest new stars was in town. He decided
that he'd like to do a gig in the UK and so he asked a taxi
driver to take him to a comedy club. The taxi driver took
him to The Comedy Store, where regulars Alexei Sayle and
Andy de la Tour agreed to Robin Williams' request that
he should play a set, so they sent him on first to warm
up the audience before the real pros did their bit. It was a
performance no one present would ever forget. He was set
to do fifteen minutes but it didn't quite work out like that.

'Forty minutes later Robin Williams walked off the

stage,' de la Tour recalled in his book *Stand-Up or Die*. 'The audience was a spent force. They were laughed out. They weren't going to laugh at anyone else probably for a year. They were draped over the chairs in a state of total exhaustion. Williams had given us a comic exhibition of such energy and imagination that "tour de force" doesn't come close.'

British audiences, it seemed, loved him just as much as those across the Atlantic. Already he had won a Grammy for his 1979 live show at the Copacabana in New York, *Reality… What A Concept* (the self-same album that Mindy was holding when she and Mork met Robin). Alongside his growing film career, he continued to make wildly popular television specials: *Off The Wall* (1978), *An Evening With Robin Williams* (1982) and *Robin Williams: Live At The Met* (1986). He was fast becoming a chat-show regular too, first appearing with David Letterman, where he put in another manic performance after becoming famous as Mork, and then with Johnny Carson. In total, he was to appear fifty times on *The Late Show with David Letterman* and the presenter was to become a friend for forty years. Letterman first saw Robin at the LA Comedy Store and remembers thinking, 'They're gonna have to put an end to show business because what can happen after this? He came in like a hurricane,' adding that he thought to himself, 'Holy crap, there goes my career in show business.' (In the event, he did OK for himself!)

But he was still intent on building up that film career,

now appearing in another disappointment, *The Survivors*, alongside Walter Matthau in 1983. 'With his new social-message comedy, *The Survivors*, starring Robin Williams and Walter Matthau, Michael Ritchie has returned to slipping whoopee cushions beneath the bottoms of smug gurus. Rude noises ensue, but the laughs are thin and scattered,' wrote James Wolcott in *Texas Monthly*. The major film success that he craved still wasn't here.

In 1983 Robin's first child, Zachary Pym 'Zak' Williams, was born. Another film followed shortly afterwards: *Moscow on the Hudson* (1984), about a Russian musician who defects to New York. It wasn't a massive hit but it did garner some positive reviews and added to the growing perception that Robin Williams was an actor to be reckoned with.

'Halfway through *The World According to Garp*, I began to think Robin Williams might need weights in his shoes to keep from floating in the air – he was that insubstantial,' wrote David Denby in *New York Magazine* in a highly positive review. 'But this time Williams is securely grounded; he has a real character to play, and he's extraordinarily touching. Bearded, and hairy as a Russian bear, he's a small, nearly innocuous figure in the Moscow scenes, clutching himself against the cold, grimacing at the sight of a three-hour waiting line for toilet paper.'

Newly sober, Williams was now a family man with a young son. He was heavily into cycling, which was to prove a life-long passion, in an effort to stay clean; just the latest sport that Robin became interested in. Previously a runner, the exercise was beginning to take its toll on his body and so he found cycling more congenial. He managed to stay sober for the best part of two decades before there was a relapse. Even so, those demons were never going to leave him alone for long. Just as he appeared to be calming down, there was yet another crisis in his private life, again centring on a woman but this time one who would end up taking him to court. Robin met Michelle Tish Carter, a cocktail waitress (just as Valerie had been when he met her), when he was performing at an LA comedy club called Improv. The two began an affair but this one lasted a little longer than some of the others before it went spectacularly off the rails.

In 1986 Michelle sued Robin for $6.2 million, alleging he had given her herpes without telling her he was infected with the virus. It was an ugly and embarrassing case, something Williams' lawyers dubbed 'Financial Attraction' (*Fatal Attraction*, another tale of an initial encounter that goes spectacularly badly wrong, had recently come out) and one that reflected badly on all the parties concerned. The case was eventually settled out of court, with Robin never admitting nor denying that he had the virus. Two years later, he and Valerie finally divorced, although there was another scandal attached to that too.

The nature of this trial was by no means unique at the time. This was the 1980s, when herpes and AIDS dominated the news agenda and an awful lot of sexually active adults were terrified of both. Debates had started about how much information you should give your new sexual partner and both Robin and Michelle were forced to admit publicly that neither had asked the other whether they had a communicable sexual disease. Philip Ryan, Robin's lawyer, argued that being the case, a person who doesn't ask and doesn't insist on condoms should be assumed to have taken the risk. Otherwise, he said, these cases will 'create a judicial ménage à trois' and open the courthouse 'to any forlorn lover whose affair has come to an unexpected end'.

Robin himself maintained a dignified silence on the subject of the virus but he couldn't resist hinting at recent turmoil in his act. 'And as we all know, there's THAT OTHER THING out there,' he told one audience. 'Which means we all have to use a little – condom sense. You know what a condom is? The bathing cap of love!' (Laugh.) 'A prophylactic, from the Latin *prophylactorum*, which means: strange party favours. I know you hate to put it on. In the heat of passion, you don't want to say, "Let's stop and put on a balloon."' The piece got a huge laugh.

It might be asked why, given that he publicly acknowledged a certain neediness and based his entire career around the concept of the phrase 'love me', Robin behaved so badly towards a wife who, indeed, loved him and who had now given him a son. But there is no straightforward answer to this. All that can be said is Williams was not stable – not even then, when he had given up drink and drugs. It was his manic side that fuelled his comedy but it was that same side that made him incapable of finding peace. While even his greatest fans would find it hard to excuse his behaviour, the problem was that the damage had already gone too deep. The man who craved love was hurting the woman who was supplying it – and very publicly too.

As divorce became inevitable, the work continued, this time with an adaptation of Saul Bellow's novel *Seize the Day* (1986). Again, it did perfectly well but failed to set the world on fire. 'Robin Williams is for the most part up to it,' wrote John Leonard in *New York Magazine*. 'His nervous comic energy reverses itself; looking inward, it corrodes instead of tickling. He is all pain, no smirk, eating his cigarettes, popping his pills. It is a claustrophobic performance, as it should be. We are crowded by his helplessness and hopelessness. And what, exactly, are his sins? Disappointing his father? Changing his name? Going to Hollywood? Wanting love? Not belonging? It is perhaps no wonder that Williams can't manage a cry that reconciles us to the thought of death.'

In 1985 Robin co-hosted the first Comic Relief in the States with Whoopi Goldberg and Billy Crystal – a charity to help the homeless which was based on the UK model and went on to raise upwards of $50 million – and in 1987 he went into therapy ('open-heart surgery in installments,' he quipped) and it was this that he credited with finally giving him the success he so craved. No one could have predicted it in advance – a movie about a disc jockey in a war zone? – but his considerable comedic powers, both as an actor and a stand-up, all came into play with *Good Morning, Vietnam* (1987).

Loosely based on the experiences of AFRS radio DJ Adrian Cronauer, the plot – as with the initial series of *Mork & Mindy* – could have been spun with Robin in mind for it played perfectly to his particular gifts. It involved Cronauer arriving in Saigon in 1965 to work for the Armed Forces Radio Service. His irreverent attitude quickly begins to annoy his superiors, including Sergeant Major Philip Dickerson (J.T. Walsh). However, others like him and his show, a mixture of humour and rock 'n' roll. As with *Mork & Mindy*, Williams was positively encouraged to improvise.

Cronauer meets Trinh (Chintara Sukapatana), a young Vietnamese girl, and follows her to an English language class, which he takes over. He then befriends her brother Tuan, whom he takes to a GI bar. A brawl ensues. Cronauer is reprimanded but business continues as usual until Tuan pulls him out of a bar minutes before it is destroyed by a bomb, something Cronauer reports despite orders not to. He is suspended but his replacement is a poor substitute. Cronauer continues to pursue Trinh and is finally and reluctantly persuaded to return to work after a convoy of soldiers convinces him to do an impromptu 'broadcast' for them before they go off to fight. Cronauer is sent out into the field and forced to hide in the jungle from the Vietcong; Tuan again finds him and rescues him once more. He is then unmasked as a member of the VC, which means Cronauer must leave with an honourable discharge if he goes quietly; the vindictive Dickerson is then also transferred away. Cronauer leaves and his place is taken by Garlick (Forest Whitaker).

The film was an absolute smash hit. Robin was awarded a Golden Globe for his performance and nominated for an Oscar (he didn't get it but he didn't have to wait for long), a Bafta and a Sant Jordi Award in Barcelona for Best Foreign Actor. The film itself and various members of the crew went on to win other awards. What's more, the critics loved it: 'Make no mistake about it: Mr. Williams's performance, though it's full of uproarious comedy, is the work of an accomplished actor. *Good Morning, Vietnam* is one man's tour de force,' wrote Vincent Canby in *The New York Times*. *TIME Magazine* called it 'the best military comedy since M★A★S★H'. 'From the start, the film bowls you over with excitement and for those who can latch on, it's a nonstop ride,' declared *Variety*. 'The perfect showcase for Robin Williams and his peerless abilities as a comic performer,' said Stephen Carty in *Flix Capacitor*.

Other reviews were more fulsome still. 'Levinson's serio-comedy about Vietnam is first and foremost a star vehicle for comedian Robin Williams, who gives a manic, highly charged performance as the real-life DJ Adrian Cronauer in the early years of the War,' said the American film critic and professor Emanuel Levy. 'Offering only hackneyed insights into the war, the film makes for stodgy drama. But Williams' manic monologues behind the mike are worth anybody's money,' wrote Geoff Andrew in *Time Out*. '*Good*

Morning, Vietnam proved that Robin Williams could act and be hilariously funny in the same film,' said James Plath in *Movie Metropolis*. And so it went on.

Somewhat ironically, given how much he wanted to be taken seriously as an actor, Williams himself admitted that the film was so successful because he was essentially playing himself. 'Until this role, the acting and the comedy have been pretty much separate on screen,' he told *The New York Times* in 1988. 'Barry [Levinson, the director] would say, "You don't have to be funny here." In the past I used to think, "I'll push it, I'll make it funnier."'

And he was certain that the therapy had helped him make the breakthrough. 'It allowed me to show more vulnerability, and I think the camera can catch that. I think therapy has helped me to bring out a deeper level of comedy,' he revealed. '[Success] moves you up in the food chain. It's like life in the Precambrian sea. There is a food chain of scripts, and success can give you access to better scripts.'

It was all the better, he said, as 'It's a hard movie to categorize. I mean, how do you describe the funny and the serious elements? It's a dramedy. But no! It's a midget comedy! No! It's a tragic farce – no! It's a black comedy – no! Well, what is it?'

He was pleased that Vietnam veterans liked it too. 'No one has said, "Hey, I was there in '65 and you weren't, and you can't do that movie." There's still so much ambivalence about the war because we are a country oriented toward victory, toward winning, and we weren't victorious… My draft number was 351, and they stopped taking people at 120. I was one lucky little white boy! I mean, with my draft number, it meant that you'd fight the V.C. when they came east on Mulholland Drive.'

'I probably would have joined up,' he added. 'My father was in the Navy and my brother was in the Air Force.'

Finally, he had the success he craved. To this day, *Good Morning, Vietnam* is considered one of the high points in his career.

In 1988 Robin and Valerie finally divorced. Exact details of the settlement are not known, but it is thought that she was awarded $50,000 a month for life (Williams was becoming an exceedingly rich man) and a one-off payment of more than $518,000 from a profit-sharing plan he had taken out. But there, too, the circumstances were extremely messy. 'Sure I'm happy about the movie,' he told *People*. 'But right now I'm moving through my personal life like a hemophiliac in a razor factory.' He wasn't kidding: this had been building for some time.

Marsha Garces was born on 18 June 1956 and was half Filipino. Her father, Leon Garces, had been born in Ubay, Bohol, and moved to the United States in 1929, later serving in the US Navy in the Second World War. Her mother, Ina Rachel Mattila, was Finnish. Marsha grew up in Shorewood, Wisconsin, and trained as a painter before finding work as a waitress and going through two brief marriages. And then, in 1984, she went to work for the Williams' family as a nanny for baby Zak.

Robin was experiencing various tribulations at the time as his marriage became increasingly rocky, but it is generally accepted that the relationship began around 1986, when Marsha officially became his secretary. Sometime in 1987 Robin and Valerie quietly separated, with a shared custody agreement for Zak and from then on it was, perhaps, inevitable that he and Marsha would wed. She was 'the one who makes my heart sing,' he declared.

Whatever the rights and wrongs of it, Robin was clearly extremely happy. 'Marsha is Robin's anchor,' said his friend and former co-star Pam Dawber. 'She's reality. Ground zero. She's very sane, and that's what he needs. She's incredibly loving too. And protective. She knows who is bad for him and who is good, and she helps keep the good relationships going.'

And she was there with him in Thailand for the filming of *Good Morning, Vietnam*. Producer Mark Johnson said, 'She was the hardest-working person on the set. She was there for him 24 hours a day. She truly loves him.' Marsha was also there for him when, in 1987, Robin's father died. The pair may have had a difficult relationship but the loss of a parent is always traumatic and Robin needed all her support.

Of course, there was also a child in the picture and so everyone was trying to be as civilised as possible. 'He's just wonderful,' said Robin in a 1988 interview with *People* magazine, 'the most sobering and wonderful thing in my life. Blond. Valerie's blue eyes. My chin. Full lips. He looks like an Aryan poster child. He has a very fertile imagination and he loves numbers. Sometimes he's like a forty-year-old Jewish accountant. Sometimes he's like Damien in *The Omen*. Sometimes he's like an angel without wings. He knows what he's feeling at all times. Today I took him to a diner for lunch. It was noisy and he doesn't like noise. "We must come back some time," he said tactfully, "when it's not so crowded." And he's not Mr. Outdoors. When I took him camping, he said, "We've got to find a room with a full refrigerator."'

But how was Zak coping with everything now? 'He's amazingly adaptive,' insisted Robin, 'and we all try hard to make the arrangement work. We all love Zachary, and Zachary loves us all. Also, we're all in therapy, and that's helped a lot – Jesus, I should get a discount! Valerie and I have a good understanding too. The separation was difficult, but it was also gentle. Better to do that than to go at each other's throats.'

Valerie concurred. 'Robin has been conducting himself very well,' she told *People*. 'We're acting together in Zach's interest. We separated to reexamine our lives. It's a time for personal growth for both of us. I see another man' – the journalist David Sheff – 'but I live alone, and I like it that way.'

And so the divorce went through but however civilised everyone involved was being, there was criticism in some quarters. Over time, Robin attempted to dispel a certain notion once and for all. 'Marsha did not break up my

Be at Peace
Sweet Robin,
You will always be
loved and remembered.

Robin Williams
1951-2014

As news of Robin Williams' shocking death spread around the world,
Broadway's lights were dimmed and Times Square paid tribute to the star.

Above: Pam Dawber and Williams shot to fame starring in the popular show
Mork and Mindy. Williams' typically zany performances – here seen in a
woman's bathrobe, furry hat and sunglasses – showcased both his acting and his
comedy skills.
© *Getty Images*

Below: The actor was married to Valerie Velardi for a decade but the couple
struggled to maintain their private relationship while Williams' career was so
public.
© *The LIFE Picture Collection/Getty Images*

Above: A Golden Globes regular, Williams was respected by both his peers and the critics, winning five individual awards through the years, culminating in the Cecil B DeMille award – one of the most coveted in the industry – for 'outstanding contributions to the world of entertainment'.

© *The LIFE Picture Collection/Getty Images*

Below: Alongside then-newcomers Affleck and Damon; *Good Will Hunting* – recognised as one of Williams' finest performances of all-time – won three Oscars.

© *AFP/Getty Images*

No matter what else may have been happening in Williams' life, his family – and especially his three children – were always at the front of his mind; not least because of the comedic potential fatherhood brought to his stand-up act.

Above: Never one to take himself too seriously, Williams is 'gunged' for Nickelodeon in 2006
© *FilmMagic*

Below left: Christopher Reeve – Williams' one-time schoolmate and great friend – said that it was the actor's antics that cheered him after his tragic accident. They were 'closer than brothers' and his death affected Williams deeply.
© *FilmMagic*

Below right: An improvisational genius, Williams often came up with his own lines for his movie roles, whether as the Genie in *Aladdin*, or in his breakthrough performance in the brilliant *Good Morning, Vietnam*.
© *AFP/Getty Images*

Above left: A stellar cast performed alongside Williams in the animated comedy *Happy Feet*, one of the more successful films of his later career.   © *WireImage*

Above right: A chat-show favourite, Williams signs autographs before appearing once again on his old friend David Letterman's *Late Show* in 2013.   © *FilmMagic*

Below: Truly comfortable live on-stage, Williams' off-screen talents were recognised at The Comedy Awards in 2012 where he received The Stand-Up Icon award.   © *FilmMagic*

Williams had found happiness in recent years with Susan Schneider, who he married in 2011.
© *FilmMagic*

Above: Never one to hold back – Williams pulls a typically energetic pose during his 2012 stand-up performance at the Stand Up For Heroes show in New York.

Below: A fallen star; shortly after Williams' death was publicly announced, his star on Hollywood's Walk of Fame was flooded with tributes to the great actor and comedian.

first marriage,' he told another interviewer. 'It was broken in shambles before we fell in love and Valerie had already found someone else. Marsha is the one who put my life back together. She's a gentle, great soul,' he told the *LA Times*.

Fresh from the success of *Good Morning, Vietnam*, Williams took part in what can only be seen, in retrospect, as a very bad idea. But it is also possible to see why it had briefly looked so good on paper. In November 1988 he and that other fine actor and comic Steve Martin starred in Samuel Beckett's classic play *Waiting For Godot*, at the Lincoln Center in New York. Directed by Mike Nichols, it was a seven-week run that sold out so quickly the tickets never even went on sale to the public. Financially, at least, it was a success.

The reasoning was obvious: two great comics who were also actors taking part in a darkly comic play about the uselessness of human existence; two tramps waiting for Godot, who never actually arrives. And there were plenty of precedents for this: it was not uncommon for huge Hollywood stars to take part in low-key stage productions, if nothing other than to prove they could. They tended to accept extremely small salaries as well, mainly to show that they were prepared to suffer for their art (and that they didn't need the money!). But if there was one playwright you should not attempt to improvise, it is Samuel Beckett, whose every comma is carefully thought out in advance. And that is where Williams went wrong.

The critics were merciless. 'But their frustrated yearning

to be recognized and their sense of life as perpetual diminishment should seem universal,' wrote William A. Henry III in *TIME Magazine*. 'Instead, the supreme existentialist tragedy of the 20th century has been reduced to a heartwarming revue sketch about the homeless. The chief sinner is Williams. When the slave Lucky makes a long, anguished speech, a flux of debased knowledge, Williams enacts the audience's presumed boredom at having to think. He scampers. He pounds the ground. He thrusts a big bone into the slave's hands as though it were an Oscar and tells him to "thank the Academy." As Martin feigns death, Williams hovers over him, murmuring the pet name "Didi, Didi," then segues into the theme from *The Twilight Zone*. Martin is never so outrageous, but his familiar cool-guy strut and laid-back vocalisms keep him from inhabiting his character.' Ouch!

'The play has new lines written into it, all vulgarisms and quite uncalled for,' fumed John Simon in *New York Magazine*. 'Many are spoken by Vladimir and Estragon during Lucky's monologue to discourage the speaker. Coyote jawbones become a movie clapper in Estragon's hands, or Yorick's skull as this gung ho Gogo, Robin Williams, mutters a Hamletic "Alas!" He also wields a large bone with words appropriate to an Oscar presentation, and goes through his usual vocal routines, doing a buzzer on a TV game show, a takeoff on the *Twilight Zone* menace music, and all sorts of trick voices, as if this were *Good Morning, Godot.*' Double ouch!

'Turning Beckett's feast of agnostic irony into a series of

revue sketches threatened to make Godot no more than a vehicle for Martin's and Williams' favourite routines,' snapped W. J. Weatherby in the *Guardian*. 'Steve Martin in a film recently turned Cyrano de Bergerac into a contemporary American with a long nose and he has now done much the same with Vladimir. As Mike Nichols did not stride on stage to demand what the hell Williams was doing, his improvisations presumably had the director's approval. But one wonders if there will be any negative reaction when news reaches the author in Paris.'

Frank Lipsius from the *Financial Times* was a little kinder. 'But does the nonchalance of their hip and cynical generation do justice to Beckett?' he wrote. 'The answer is yes, despite liberties the author would no doubt look askance at, since he is a notorious purist about productions of his plays. There is only one false note, at the end of Act One, when Robin Williams as Estragon groans unnecessarily as the lights go down on their inability to move. Yet throughout the production Williams does a complete pantomime with only slight reference to the text. When Vladimir hurriedly exits, Williams stares after him, laughingly lifting his leg and scratching the ground like a dog. He picks up a steer skull and addresses it like Hamlet or moves the jaws like a ventriloquist. To get Lucky to stop talking he shouts out "You're a liberal!" in a mocking reference to the presidential campaign.

Williams, newly covered in glory from *Good Morning, Vietnam*, and Martin, were unaccustomed to such a reaction.

It clearly hurt and, some years later, Robin returned to the subject. 'Painful,' he told *Playboy*. 'We put our ass out and got kicked for it. Some nights I would improvise a bit and hard-core Beckett fans got pissed off. We played it as a comedy team, it wasn't existential. Like these two guys from vaudeville who would go into routines that would fall apart into angst. Basically, it's Laurel and Hardy, which is how Beckett staged it in Germany.'

But he didn't need to worry. After a tumultuous few years of drying out, divorce, law suits, remarriage and then, finally, the hit movie for which he'd been waiting so long, Robin Williams was still one of the hottest names on the planet. He had the pick of the scripts in front of him now – everyone wanted a piece of him and was clamouring to sign him up. He would go on to make plenty of dud films, lapsing far too much into the sentimental but, for now, he was on a roll. And his finest hour was still to come.

'Goooooooood morning, Vietnam! It's 0600 hours.
What does the "O" stand for? O my God, it's early!
Speaking of early, let's hear it for that Marty Lee Drywitz.
Silky-smooth sounds, making me sound like Peggy Lee...'

ADRIAN CRONAUER (ROBIN WILLIAMS),

GOOD MORNING, VIETNAM (1987)

CHAPTER EIGHT

IN HIS PRIME

'O Captain! My Captain!'
DEAD POETS SOCIETY (1989)

The debacle of *Waiting for Godot* aside, the late 1980s and early 1990s saw Robin Williams at the peak of his profession, producing arguably his finest work. It was as if *Good Morning, Vietnam* had opened the floodgates: after some years in which it had seemed he would not, after all, achieve his potential, now the successes were flooding in thick and fast. He was to make over sixty films in total, some of them unforgettable or – worse in some eyes – far too sentimental but the most noteworthy rank right up there with the best films ever. And *Dead Poets Society* (1989) is unquestionably one of them.

Directed by Peter Weir, with a script by Tom Schulman, and set in the Welton Academy in 1959, the film depicts the story of an inspirational teacher, John Keating (Williams), who turns accepted teaching methods on their head. His students – Neil Perry (Robert Sean Leonard), Todd Anderson (Ethan Hawke), Knox Overstreet (Josh Charles), Charlie Dalton (Gale Hansen), Richard Cameron (Dylan Kussman), Steven Meeks (Allelon Ruggiero) and Gerard Pitts (James Waterston) – may call him 'O Captain! My Captain!' he tells them, a reference to a Walt Whitman poem. He then persuades them to rip out the introduction to their poetry textbook!

On discovering that Keating is himself a former alumnus, the boys revive a club, the Dead Poets Society, to which Keating once belonged, which meets in secret. Meanwhile, Keating is encouraging them all to discover their inner potential, helping Anderson with a writing assignment. Dalton publishes an article saying that girls should be admitted to the school and is punished as a result. Overstreet falls in love and woos his girl with poetry. Perry wants to be an actor and takes part in a production of *A Midsummer Night's Dream* against the express wishes of his father, who confronts Keating before withdrawing his son from the school and telling him he will go to Harvard and have a career in medicine. Perry subsequently commits suicide.

An investigation is launched, during which Cameron puts the blame on Keating and reveals the existence of the Dead Poets Society. Dalton punches him and is duly expelled. Headmaster Nolan (Norman Lloyd) calls Anderson to his office, forces him to admit to belonging to the society and then makes him sign a document that blames Keating for encouraging Perry to flout his father's wishes. Keating is then fired.

Nolan takes over the English class, discovers the introduction to the poetry book is missing and, as he finds one undamaged book for a boy to read from, Keating enters the class to reclaim a few possessions. Anderson tells him that he was forced to sign the document and, as Nolan orders him to be silent, climbs on his desk and shouts 'O Captain! My Captain!', Nolan tells him that, if he doesn't sit down, he will be expelled. The rest of the boys ignore him and climb onto their desks, looking to Keating. Very much moved, he leaves, having changed the boys' lives and made them aware of their own potential.

A touching story (even if it managed to imply that individuality and inspirational teaching will get you the sack if you're the teacher and cause death if you're the student), it was one of the greatest successes of Williams' career. The critics were almost united in their praise: the *Washington Post*'s reviewer called it 'solid, smart entertainment' and praised Robin for giving a 'nicely restrained acting performance'. Vincent Canby of *The New York Times* wrote of his 'exceptionally fine performance' and pointed out that '*Dead Poets Society* is far less about Keating than about a handful of impressionable boys'. Pauline Kael wasn't sure about the film's 'middlebrow high-mindedness' but praised the lead: 'Robin Williams' performance is more graceful than anything he's done before – he's totally, concentratedly there – [he] reads his lines stunningly, and when he mimics various actors reciting Shakespeare there's no undue clowning in it; he's a gifted teacher demonstrating his skills.'

Roger Ebert was more cautious, worrying that Williams' comic persona spilled into the acting and talked of a 'collection of pious platitudes … The movie pays lip service to qualities and values that, on the evidence of the screenplay itself, it is cheerfully willing to abandon.'

Awards began flooding in. *Dead Poets Society* won the Oscar for Best Original Screenplay, while Williams, director Peter Weir and the film itself were all awarded Oscar nominations. Various Bafta awards and nominations followed, alongside citations from around the world. The famous line 'Carpe diem. Seize the day, boys. Make your life extraordinary,' was voted the ninety-fifth greatest movie quote by the American Film Institute. Even the title was vindicated – there had been concerns that it would be a difficult one to sell to the public, with actor and producer Harrison Ford saying the only worse title he could think of would have been *Dead Poets Society in Winter* – but it had worked.

Peter Weir revealed that he'd had to keep Williams on a tight leash. 'Keating's humor had to be part of the personality,' he told *Premiere* magazine in 1989. 'Robin and I agreed at the start that he was not going to be an entertainer in the classroom. That would have been wrong for the film as a whole. It would have been so easy for him to have the kids rolling on the floor, doubled up with laughter. So he had to put the brakes on at times.' However, he did allow the actor to run loose in the Shakespeare scene: 'I had two cameras going, obviously, and I just said, "Boys, this is not a scripted scene. Treat Robin as your teacher and react accordingly, and don't forget that it's 1959."' Another innovation on Weir's part was to gather the seven young actors who played the students together and get them to play sports before filming even began in order to create a bond between them that was essential for the movie.

Meanwhile, Robin, the acknowledged hero of the hour, was walking on air. His personal life was looking up too: on 30 April 1989 he married Marsha and she gave birth to his daughter, Zelda Rae Williams, shortly afterwards. Famously, Zelda was named after Princess Zelda of 'The Legend of Zelda' video-game series – Robin was a very keen gamer up to the end of his life, so much so that some people thought it might have contributed to his depression – although he later said that it was Zak's idea. But he was very happy about it. The couple's second child, Cody Alan Williams, arrived in 1991.

Robin was now involved in a set of films that were making headlines. Next up was *Awakenings* (1990), the true story of the British neurologist Oliver Sacks – turned into an American called Malcolm Sayer (Williams) in the movie – who discovers that the drug L-dopa (also known as levodopa) can be used to treat those who survived the 1917–28 epidemic of Encephalitis Lethargica (EL). Patients, including Leonard Lowe, who was played by Robert De Niro, were awakened after decades of catatonia. It was directed by Penny Marshall, John Belushi's old friend.

While a difficult subject, the general consensus was that it was treated with a good deal of taste. The film began with Sayer discovering that some patients could respond to certain types of stimuli: when a ball is thrown at them, for example, or when they hear familiar music. Leonard is reached by means of an Ouija board. Gradually, the patients start coming back to life and, as he does so, Leonard becomes romantically interested in the daughter of another patient, as well as beginning to chafe against the restrictions the hospital places on him and causing some disruption in the process. But then his body once more starts to disintegrate and everyone realises that the effect of the drug is only temporary. In the only slight hint of mawkishness in the film, 'awakenings' is taken to have a different meaning as Sayer, a chronically shy man, asks a nurse out for coffee and the medical staff begin to treat the patients, once more catatonic, with greater respect.

There was another flood of good reviews. 'After seeing *Awakenings*, I read it, to know more about what happened in that Bronx hospital,' wrote Roger Ebert in the *Chicago Sun-Times*. 'What both the movie and the book convey is the immense courage of the patients and the profound experience of their doctors, as in a small way they re-experienced what it means to be born, to open your eyes and discover to your astonishment that "you" are alive.'

'*Awakenings* has been made with sensitivity and taste,' wrote David Denby in *New York Magazine*. 'There is certainly no exploitation of the obvious sort, and nothing in the sensational, brazen style of *One Flew Over the Cuckoo's Nest* (the high reputation of that ideological nuthatch bash amazes me). The patients are always treated as people, not as spectacle, though in fact the strangeness and the stress of their clinical symptoms are the most arresting things in the movie... As concocted by screenwriter Steven Zaillian, Sayer needs awakening himself. Timid and guarded, kindly yet cut off and asexual, he is a man with a vital element missing. Williams, having dropped the adorable Pied Piper act that made his performances in *Good Morning, Vietnam* and *Dead Poets Society* so tiresome, does some serious work. Masked by a fuzzy beard, he holds his arms at his side and hunches slightly, as if he were trying to stop cold air from sliding up his tummy.'

Other critics were won over, albeit with reservations. 'There's a raw, subversive element in De Niro's performance: he doesn't shrink from letting Leonard seem grotesque,' said Owen Gleiberman of *Entertainment Weekly*. 'Yet *Awakenings*, unlike the infinitely superior *Rain Man*, isn't really built around the quirkiness of its lead character. The movie views Leonard piously; it turns him into an icon of feeling. And so even if you're held (as I was) by the acting, you may find yourself fighting the film's design.'

Oliver Sacks, however, author of the 1973 memoir on which the film is based, 'was pleased with a great deal ...

I think in an uncanny way, De Niro did somehow feel his way into being Parkinsonian. So much so that sometimes when we were having dinner afterwards, I would see his foot curl or he would be leaning to one side, as if he couldn't seem to get out of it. I think it was uncanny the way things were incorporated. At other levels I think things were sort of sentimentalized and simplified somewhat.'

But he loved Williams' performance. 'Robin has an almost instant access to parts of the mind – dreamlike parts, with phantasmagoric associations – that most of us don't,' he told *New York Magazine*. 'Robin becoming other people reminds me of Theodore Hook, the early-nineteenth-century wit who could improvise operas, playing every part. He was the most popular man in London, constantly invited out to dinner and to perform. For Hook, as for Robin, the demand never let up. But Hook never had a chance for quiet inwardness – he drank heavily, and he died in his fifties. Robin's brilliance, however, is considerably controlled. He's not in its grip.' It was a somewhat prescient comment in light of what was to happen two and a half decades on.

But the admiration was mutual, with Robin citing this role as his favourite ever in his 2013 interview on *Reddit*. 'I think playing Oliver Sacks in *Awakenings* was a gift because I got to meet him, and got to explore the human brain from the inside out,' he said. 'Because Oliver writes about human behavior subjectively and that for me was the beginning of a fascination with human behavior.'

Meanwhile, the reviewers were still having their say and Desson Howe of the *Washington Post* was not so impressed, saying, 'when [Sayers' love interest] nurse Julie Kavner (another former TV being) delivers the main Message (life, she tells Williams, is "given and taken away from all of us"), it doesn't sound like the climactic point of a great movie. It sounds more like a line from one of the more sensitive episodes of *Laverne & Shirley*.'

Janet Maslin of *The New York Times* said, '*Awakenings* works harder at achieving such misplaced liveliness than at winning its audience over in other ways.'

Williams was, by now, widely considered to be an outstanding actor but his next choice jarred with many: playing a grown-up Peter Pan in *Hook* (1991). It is conceivably possible that the reason he accepted the role was because he'd never actually seen a production of the play: he did so for the first time at the age of thirty-eight after director Steven Spielberg had already signed him up. It has a sensational cast – Dustin Hoffman (Captain Hook), Julia Roberts (Tinkerbell), Bob Hoskins (Smee) and Maggie Smith (Granny Wendy) but the conceit, that Peter has grown up and as Peter Banning, a corporate lawyer with a wife and two children, has forgotten his own childhood, was too much for some. The villainous Hook kidnaps his family and Peter must go back to Neverland to rescue them, but the story just didn't come off. The film was a commercial success (though not as successful as forecast) but a critical failure and, in a career of hits and misses, this one definitely fell into the latter camp.

This unexpected flop was almost immediately compensated for when Williams made what some people consider to be his finest film: *The Fisher King* (1991). Directed by Terry Gilliam and written by Richard LaGravenese, it was a fantasy offering that could easily have lost its way but did not. It concerned Jack Lucas (Jeff Bridges), a shock jock whose on-air utterances prompt someone to commit mass murder in a Manhattan bar. Lucas becomes a hopeless drunk, working in a record store with his girlfriend Anne, before being attacked by a group of thugs. He is rescued by Parry (Williams), a homeless man looking for the Holy Grail. Initially, Jack is cautious but then discovers that Parry had been rendered catatonic for a time after seeing his wife murdered by the same psycho who carried out the bar killing (and had previously called Lucas). Parry is haunted by a hallucination of a Red Knight, of which he is terrified. He tells Jack the story of the Fisher King, who was charged with guarding the Holy Grail.

Jack wants to redeem himself for inadvertently having caused the killings. He introduces Parry to Lydia (Amanda Plummer), an accountant who Parry has a crush on, and they fall in love. But Parry sees the Red Knight and flees, only to run into the same thugs who had gone after Jack. They beat him and he returns to a catatonic state. To help him, Jack breaks into the house of a famous architect and takes possession of a simple trophy that Parry believes to be the Grail: in so doing, he prevents the suicide of the architect by tripping the alarm. He takes the trophy to Parry, who regains consciousness and is reunited with Lydia. Finally, Jack tells Anne he loves her and they embrace.

This was not one of Williams' major box-office successes, although it performed perfectly respectably, but the critics loved it. '*The Fisher King* has two actors at the top of their form, and a compelling, well-directed and well-produced story,' said *Variety*. 'Visually impressive, frequently pretentious, and extremely fluid as narrative (the 137 minutes sail by effortlessly), this mythic comedy-drama presents Gilliam as half seer, half snake-oil salesman and defies you to sort out which is which,' wrote Jonathan Rosenbaum in the *Chicago Reader*. 'Although there are moments when the mixture of comedy, fantasy and drama don't come off, this is still an original, touching movie that is well worth the price of a ticket,' opined Jo Berry in *Empire Magazine*.

'Working within the constraints of a big studio film has brought out Gilliam's best: he's become a true storyteller and a wonderful director of actors. This time he delights not only the eye but the soul,' said David Ansen in *Newsweek*. 'A touching and funny one-of-a-kind gem about two lost souls who help each other find redemption. Bridges once again proves what an underappreciated actor he is, while Williams is at his manic best,' said Chuck O'Leary of *FulvueDrive-In.com*. '*The Fisher King* emphasizes the purpose of fairy tales in our lives, and the way a fantasy can help us see reality more clearly,' said Jeffrey Overstreet.

The film resulted in another Oscar nomination for

Williams (who, by now, must have been feeling always the bridesmaid, never the bride), while his co-star Mercedes Ruehl, who played Anne, won the Oscar for Best Supporting Actress, as well as a number of other awards. There was a score of further Oscar nominations for the movie and the usual international suspects, with Williams getting a Golden Globe Award for Best Actor on the back of his performance. Terry Gilliam, meanwhile, won the People's Choice Award from the Toronto International Film Festival for what had been a stunningly original take on what was actually Arthurian legend. It was another triumph all round.

The hits and misses continued. Next up was *Toys* (1992), another fantasy film with a fine cast, including Michael Gambon, Joan Cusack, Robin Wright and Jamie Foxx in his film debut, all about a childlike man who owns a toy factory. '*Toys* is a very whimsical, strange feast, almost a nonmusical musical,' Williams told *The New York Times*. 'I hope people enjoy the ride.' But they didn't – the film was regarded as a failure, both critically and commercially, with the director Barry Levinson seen as partly to blame. Given that he had also directed *Good Morning, Vietnam* (and *Rain Man* in 1988), it was unclear why the project had gone so badly wrong.

'[What made the film] that much sadder a failure is that everyone involved must have sincerely felt they were doing the Lord's work, care and concern going hand in hand with an almost total miscalculation of mood,' said Kenneth

Turan in the *Los Angeles Times*. 'Even Robin Williams, so lively a voice in *Aladdin*, is on beatific automatic pilot here, preferring to be warm and cuddly when a little of his energy (paradoxically on splendid display in the film's teaser trailer) is desperately called for. The Grinch Who Stole Christmas seems to have stripped the life from this film as well, leaving a pretty shell, expensive but hollow, in its place.'

'To cut *Toys* a minor break, it is ambitious,' wrote Peter Travers in *Rolling Stone*. 'It is also a gimmicky, obvious and pious bore, not to mention overproduced and overlong.'

But for every miss there was a hit. Williams had, indeed, starred in the aforementioned *Aladdin* (1992), or at least voiced his part: the role of Genie/Merchant had been written specifically with him in mind – a risk, as he took a lot of persuading before he would accept. He didn't want to work for Disney, he said, with the result that two of the writers, Ron Clements and John Musker, who were also the producers and directors, created a reel of animation of the Genie, which they allied to Robin's real life stand-up. When they showed it to him, he thought it was so funny that he agreed to do the film. He also improvised a great deal of his part, contributing up to thirty hours on tape that had to be cut down to fit the movie, impersonating numerous others in the process, including Jack Nicholson, Carol Channing, Ethel Merman, William F. Buckley Jr., Robert De Niro ('Are you talkin' to me?') and Pinocchio. 'I was improvising, and the animators came in and laughed, and it just grew,' he told *New York Magazine*. 'In times like this, when there's so much crap running around, it's great to laugh and be free. I felt wonderful; that's why I did it. And it was such a pleasure when it came out and people said, "I loved it as much as my kid did." But then some things happened later on.'

A veritable tour de force, it was estimated that, in total, Williams improvised about fifty-two different voices. In the event, *Aladdin* was the most successful film of 1992.

Unusually for Robin, who was on the whole considered to be an easy person to work with, the movie generated some bad feeling on the part of all those involved because of the events that happened later on. For various reasons, related to the fact that *Toys* was coming out around the same time, Williams demanded that his name and image would not be used for marketing and would not take more than 25 per cent of marketing space. The studio did not stick to the letter of the deal, using his voice to sell merchandise of the products, leading to a very public and bitter row between the two of them, with Robin, who had taken a much smaller fee than usual (this was normal for a voiceover), refusing to do any promotion. What this essentially boiled down to was that he said he'd do the film if they didn't present it as a Robin Williams' vehicle, which they then did.

It ended in Disney publicly apologising to Robin (and giving him a Picasso then valued at $1 million and no doubt worth considerably more now) but it was an unhappy episode that left an unpleasant taste in the mouth. 'It wasn't as if we hadn't set it out,' he said. 'I don't want to sell stuff. It's the one thing I don't do. In *Mork & Mindy*, they did Mork dolls – I didn't mind the dolls; the image is theirs. But the voice, that's me; I gave them my self. When it happened, I said, "You know I don't do that." And they apologized; they said it was done by other people.'

In his spare time, Robin was still doing stand-up, an act that he pretty much imported onto his numerous chat-show appearances, which were fast becoming known as being quite as enjoyable as watching his act. In 1992 he appeared on *The Arsenio Hall Show* and spoke of it in much the same way as he did his actual act: 'Going on stage is part catharsis for me, but it's almost trying to work out my own fears,' he told *The New York Times* shortly after he returned from a trip to the UK.

The interview was also an explanation as to quite how much current affairs informed his act. 'Tonight I was jet-lagged, but I just wanted to explode with all this information,' he said of his appearance on the show. 'You want to talk about the marines in Somalia hitting the beach and meeting the press. "All right, Colonel, I want you to take out that camera position. Get away, son! He's got a flashbulb!" And, like, the royal family. I was in England and Windsor Castle was burning down and, like, it's not insured. Oh, damn, I'm sorry! Let the people pay 8 billion crowns. And there's no sprinkler system. Oh rot!'

Entertaining stuff but there was also a truly manic

quality to it – this was a newspaper interview, after all. But it seemed as if Robin just couldn't turn off the tap: something inside was relentless, pushing him to be funny even when he didn't have to be. It was the mark of a comic genius, all right – but it wasn't healthy and didn't give the impression of a man at peace with himself.

Then again, there were certainly some things he could be pretty serious about and, at that stage, Marsha was one of them. The relationship was very strong then, with Robin crediting her with pulling him through a very difficult time and he fiercely resented the picture that had been painted of him running off with the nanny. Indeed, he blamed it on a piece in *People Magazine*.

'It was an ambush by them,' he told *The New York Times* in 1992. 'It's very destructive. It still is. There are still nanny jokes. You want to go out and yell.

'There was an article about men who leave their wives when they become famous. And I wanted to write to this man and say, "Listen, you may have your ridiculous theories, but the truth is my wife left me." My marriage had been in a shambles for some time. Marsha just basically started to talk to me and said: "Listen jerk, what are you having these ridiculous affairs for? What are you yelling and screaming about? Wake up!" Slowly I began realizing I'm a decent person, and everything wonderful that has happened to my life is because of her. It's hideous that she takes the rap as a home wrecker, which is a lie. It's the exact opposite. She has taken me from zero to the sky.'

It was an unusually impassioned outburst and, for Robin to complain about anyone making jokes, when he so often mercilessly harpooned the pompous himself, showed that this had left some real scars. For him, it was yet another sign that fame had its downside: people took an interest in your private life and made remarks. Still, he was now top of the Hollywood A-list, enjoying the fruits of his success and a seriously rich man. He was about to enjoy some further career highlights in the forthcoming years – but also experience a terrible tragedy that struck one of his closest friends.

> Margaret: *Miriam, there's no easy way to tell you this, so –*
> *your husband – he was granted a divorce from you in 1952.*
> Miriam: *Oh, thank God!*
> *AWAKENINGS* (1990)

CHAPTER NINE

TRIUMPH AND TRAGEDY

'You're only given a little spark of madness,
you mustn't lose it.'
ROBIN WILLIAMS

For much of the 1990s, Williams' film career continued to soar. In 1993 there was another seminal role, this time in *Mrs. Doubtfire*, based on Anne Fine's novel *Alias Madame Doubtfire* and co-starring Sally Field. Strangely enough, when first released the film received decidedly mixed reviews but it is now considered to be one of the great classics, ranking 67th in the American Film Institute's 100 Years, 100 Laughs: America's Funniest Movies and 40th on Bravo's 100 Funniest Movies of All Time.

The film, which also starred Pierce Brosnan in his pre-Bond days, told the tale of Daniel and Miranda Hillard, divorced parents of three. Daniel, as luck would have it, is a voice actor (this gave Robin a great many opportunities to clown around) and so, after the divorce goes through and he gets extremely limited custody, he dresses up as a Scottish nanny and works his way back into his children's lives. In the end, all is revealed and he is forgiven with the message (by this time a great many of Williams' films had messages) that not only had he learned to become a better father but family triumphed above all else.

(In a rather touching example of the fact that this is actually true, a totally unknown actor called Dr. Toad had a bit part as a bartender in the movie. In actual fact, Dr. Toad was none other than R. Todd Williams, now an acclaimed wine maker and co-founder of Toad Hollow Vineyards and Robin's oldest half-brother. He had, indeed, been a bartender in his time.)

And Williams certainly managed to pull it off: his performance was absolutely central to the movie. 'In the film, if Robin's character doesn't fool the woman he'd been married to for fourteen years, she won't hire him – and there'd be no movie,' director Chris Columbus told *New York Magazine* in 1993. But it was far more personal than many people realised: Robin himself had recently been through a divorce and was well aware of all the problems caused when parents and children don't see enough of each other. In some ways, this was as raw as the stand-up material he had once done about taking drugs.

Mrs. Doubtfire was much compared to *Tootsie* (1982), the

Dustin Hoffman vehicle in which he, too, dragged up in order to get work in a soap opera but, while that film was deservedly and immediately recognised as a comic classic, *Mrs. Doubtfire* was not. It was compared, on the whole unfavourably, with another of the cross-dressing greats, *Some Like It Hot* (1959) and, even the (sort of) complimentary reviews were a little sharp.

'I've rarely laughed so much at a movie I generally disliked,' said David Ansen in *Newsweek*. 'The dress, the mask and Mrs. Doubtfire's gentility are inherently limiting, but nothing holds Mr. Williams back when he's on a roll,' wrote Janet Maslin in *The New York Times*. 'Although overly sappy in places and probably twenty minutes too long, this Robin Williams-in-drag vehicle provides the comic a slick surface for doing his shtick, within a story possessing broad family appeal,' opined Brian Lowry in *Variety*.

'Sit-com stuff, then, with laboured farcical interludes, and a mushy post-feminist sensibility. Funny notwithstanding,' came from Derek Adams in *Time Out*. 'Williams has to break out of a second-rate *Tootsie* imitation, ankles clamped in pathos and face covered in latex. He pulls it off in the end, but it's not pretty,' said Desson Thomson in the *Washington Post*. And, much more positively and also from the *Washington Post*, 'You will laugh till your ribs ache – not because director Chris Columbus of the *Home Alone* movies has a gift for farce, which he does, but because Williams is to funny what the Energizer Bunny is to batteries. He keeps going and going and going,' said Rita Kempley.

But the people who really knew about these things – namely the film industry – immediately recognised its quality. Williams won the Global Globe Award for Best Actor for his performance and the movie got Best Film. It also won an Oscar, although admittedly for Best Make-up. Robin was certainly taking it seriously.

'Here's a guy who lives in a very random way and, through a painful process, finds there's more than him,' he told *New York Magazine*. 'And the wife, she does the same thing. We had an early go with the studio; they wanted the couple to get back together. Well, that's the one fantasy most psychiatrists will tell you is perpetuated by children of divorce who are in therapy – and it's the one thing that professionals don't want to perpetuate. They'll ask kids, "Ever have a memory of your mom and dad together?" The kids say no, but it's the grand concept: "They're together. Sold to you by Norman Rockwell. The family, at the table ... even though they're all armed." This movie is about real family values. After a divorce, how many fathers just give up? The tendency is to say, "I love my son," and then pull away. If you're lucky, the father becomes an uncle. But the weird thing is, he needs his kids as much as they need him.'

Mrs. Doubtfire was to become one of his major successes, so much so that there was talk of a sequel (Robin actually disliked sequels) right up to the end of his life. Various plot ideas were mentioned, including disguising himself as a woman to look for his daughter when she went to college, but nothing ever seemed quite right. Then in later years, when Williams' career was, perhaps, not quite so stratospheric as it had once been, there was even talk that another *Mrs. Doubtfire* might rescue it. But it was not to be.

Even as late as May 2013, however, the director Chris Columbus was still talking about the possibility. '[Robin Williams and I are] talking about a sequel to *Mrs. Doubtfire*,' he said in an interview with the *Huffington Post*. 'We've talked about it, and the studio is interested in it. The thing that fascinates me about a sequel to *Mrs. Doubtfire* is with most actors who create an iconic character like Mrs. Doubtfire, when you come back and do that character, well, you're twenty years older so you're not going to look the same. The cool thing with Mrs. Doubtfire is there's a character, there's a woman, who is actually going to look exactly as she did in 1993. So I look forward to seeing that trailer. I love that concept and there's no CGI. So we just need to make absolutely certain that the story is a good emotionally strong story, that there's a reason for telling it, it's not like *Big Momma's House* or something. It has to be as emotional and as funny.'

Back in 1993 Robin was finding a way of living with his now massive fame. That summer he took his family off to a villa in Italy for a while and completely cut himself off from the business. They were also about to move to a huge 12,000-foot estate overlooking the San Francisco Bay. Still very much enmeshed as a family, Marsha was, by now, playing a pivotal role in Williams' career: understanding his vulnerability, she acted as a kind of 'gatekeeper' to him, protecting him from as much of the pressures of the industry as she could.

And she did a great deal more than that: before *Good Morning, Vietnam,* she encouraged Robin to study the history of the era. She was on the set of most of his films, providing back-up and support. Sometimes she sounded as much like his agent as anything else: 'Money's never been the reason for me to recommend anything,' she told *New York Magazine.* 'Unless the entire country collapses, we have as much as we'll ever need. I'm more interested in looking at what Robin hasn't done and seeing what's next. I'm prejudiced, but I've never seen anyone with his range.'

While some people sniped that she was becoming a pushy Hollywood wife, it was actually ideal for Robin. The two of them set up the Blue Wolf production company to vet scripts and find suitable projects for him and it was Marsha who came across *Mrs. Doubtfire.* She was actually the producer on the film, again raising eyebrows but, given everything she did was designed to boost the status and happiness of her husband, not for the first time the doubters got it wrong. She would go on to produce further films for him too.

But while all was happy enough at that stage on the home front, one of Robin's closest friends was to shortly experience a major tragedy. Christopher Reeve, his old mucker from the Juilliard days, was now just as famous, although in a totally different way, having made his name in the *Superman* films. An intensely athletic and energetic man, one of his hobbies was riding but, in June 1995, he was thrown from his horse and landed on his head. He broke his neck and, from that moment until the end of his life, nine years later, he was paralysed from the neck down.

It was, of course, an utterly devastating event for everyone involved, above all Reeve and his wife Dana. He later confessed to feeling suicidal (and who could blame him?) but, with the encouragement of his wife, resolved to carry on as best he could. In later years, he remembered nothing of the accident and was initially delirious; he was then subjected to an operation to reattach his skull to his spine, for which there was only a 50 per cent chance of survival. Even a man as unquestionably brave as Reeve would have been beside himself: in the run-up to the operation, a 'squat fellow' burst in wearing scrubs and glasses and talking in a Russian accent. He was going to give Reeve a rectal examination, he said. It was, of course, Williams, replaying a minor role he'd had in the Hugh Grant 1995 vehicle *Nine Months* and Christopher burst out laughing, the first time he'd done so since the accident. 'My old friend had helped me know that somehow I was going to be ok,' he later wrote in his autobiography *Still Me*.

'Christopher Reeve and I went to Julliard together. When I learned of his accident I was as devastated as everyone else,' Robin later told the *Calgary Sun*. 'People were so solemn. I knew it was not good for Chris, so I dressed up in hospital scrubs and pretended to be his proctologist. The smile on his face almost broke my heart. He has told me since that it was at that moment when he was able to laugh again that he wanted to live.'

But Robin did far more than just make Christopher laugh. It has never been made public to what extent this happened but it was widely rumoured that he had contributed to the cost of Reeve's medical care. Certainly he became involved in the Christopher & Dana Reeve Foundation. Dana described the two of them as being 'closer than brothers' and, as the years went by, Robin was often seen at his old friend's side. Reeve's tragic physical transformation spoke volumes of the life he had left behind.

In fact, behind the scenes Robin did a huge amount for charity. He supported, among others, Comic Relief (for the homeless and Hurricane Katrina victims), Médecins Sans Frontières, Operation Smile, the Pediatric AIDS Association, Challenged Athletes Foundation, St. Jude Children's Research Hospital, the Make-a-Wish Foundation (some of the children were in *Patch Adams*, 1998), Project Open Hand, Glide, The Gorilla Foundation, Seacology, River of Words, God's Love We Deliver, Women at Ground Zero, Bread and Roses, Meridian Gallery, Mercury House, Kidsclub, Season of Sharing, SMMoA, Ant Farm, Fresno County Public Library, Muir Fest, USO, Best Friends, the University of California, San Francisco (UCSF) and San Francisco General Hospital Pediatrics.

He was also a frequent visitor to children's wards in San Francisco hospitals. 'I usually go at Christmas,' he told the *Calgary Sun*. 'I ride a bike hooked up to an IV. I used to be a real hit when I did Mork but now they love it most when I break into Mrs. Doubtfire.'

His motivation was completely different from so many celebrities who do good works mainly to feed in to their own PR. Williams had come from a wealthy background anyway and now he was stratospherically wealthy (it was estimated that in the course of just two years in the early 1990s he earned $29 million, which was worth even more then than it is today). And he went far beyond what so many others do. He made benefit appearances to support literacy and women's rights and performed a great deal on the United Service Organizations (USO), which looked after the entertainment of American troops abroad. In total, he was to visit 13 countries for the USO, including Iraq and Afghanistan, entertaining 100,000 troops. (In this he was like one of the other great American comedy actors, Bob Hope, also a regular with the United States Army.)

Along with Marsha, he founded the Windfall Foundation for many charities and he continued with this activity for the rest of his life. In December 1999 he sang in French on the BBC-inspired music video of international celebrities doing a cover of The Rolling Stones' 'It's Only Rock 'n Roll (But I Like It)' for the charity Children's Promise. After the 2010 Canterbury earthquake, Williams donated all proceeds of his *Weapons of Self Destruction* Christchurch performance to help rebuild the New Zealand city (half the proceeds were donated to the Red Cross and half to the mayoral building fund). He was also a supporter of St.

Jude Children's Research Hospital. After he died, many of the people and charities to whom he had given support came forward to praise him: even his worst detractors had to concede that he was an exceptionally generous man.

And the films kept rolling on out. Some sank without a trace but others became part of the cultural landscape: *Jumanji*, for example, a 1995 offering that had twelve-year-old Alan Parrish (Williams) trapped in a strange board game called Jumanji in 1969 and only being released twenty-six years later as an adult when two more children start playing the game. But when he gets out, so too do all the monsters and the terror that were hiding in there with him. Interestingly, given Robin's sometimes fraught relationship with his own father, the actor who portrays his father in the film and later the crazed hunter out to get him are one and the same man: something no one comments on at any stage. Williams would surely have seen the irony in that.

The film earned both mixed reviews and a great deal of money, which meant that anyone upset by the critics was at least able to cry all the way to the bank. And it was good, old-fashioned fun. 'A machete. Flamethrower! And a nightlight (oh, that's right, I was ten, so maybe I should lose the flamethrower and exchange that for a Ronson lighter),' said Williams on *Reddit* when asked what he'd have taken if he had to go into the board game that was Jumanji.

And some of the critics were prepared to accept the fun element. 'Take away the CGI mayhem and what emerges is a rather touching tale of second chances and innocence prematurely lost,' said Neil Smith on *BBC.com*. 'A calculated but very entertaining special effects extravaganza,' declared *USA Today*. 'Like the rest of Johnston's oeuvre, *Jumanji* puts vivid characters through paces that will quicken any child's pulse,' said Peter Canavese in *Groucho Reviews*.

'A visually impressive and exhilarating adventure that keeps the suspense, thrills and comedy running high through the surprising end and supplies interesting characters with moving plights that keep the audience rooting,' declared Christine James in *Boxoffice Magazine*. 'Everyone is good here, with Williams taking on the unusual persona of straightman much of the way,' said Chris Hicks in *Deseret News*. Audiences loved it too, with Williams as a sort of Indiana Jones character, albeit not an archaeologist looking for lost treasures but just an ordinary Joe.

But the famous film critic Roger Ebert was less than impressed: 'The movie itself is likely to send younger children fleeing from the theater, or hiding in their parents' arms. Those who do sit all the way through it are likely to toss and turn with nightmares inspired by its frightening images,' he wrote in the *Chicago Sun-Times*. 'Whoever thought this was a family movie (the MPAA rates it PG – not even PG-13!) must think kids are made of stern stuff. The film is a gloomy special-effects extravaganza filled with grotesque images, generating fear and despair. Even for older audiences, there are few redeeming factors, because what little story there is serves as a coathook for the f/x sequences, which come out of nowhere and evaporate into the same place.'

149

Despite this, *Jumanji* has gone on to become one of the acknowledged famous children's films and is still a firm favourite on television, where it is regularly screened.

Williams was a busy man. In 1996 there was *The Birdcage*, based on the French smash hit *La Cage aux Folles*, about a gay couple: Armand Goldman (Williams), who owns a nightclub, and his partner Albert (Nathan Lane), a drag queen. (Many people expressed surprise that the casting wasn't the other way around.) Armand has a son, Val (Dan Futterman), who has just got engaged and wants to introduce the two sets of parents but his fiancée comes from conservative stock. Much hilarity ensues.

Were they worried they were putting across a somewhat stereotypical view of gays, with a lot of screeching and camp? 'The one thing that will help is the tenderness of it,' Robin told *Premiere* magazine. 'We may have sacrificed something, but we tried to get across a couple who were just as loving as any heterosexual couple. It's a love story. But you have to brace yourself, though, because there's gonna be people pissed off.'

It also put him in the very unusual position of being the one to tone it down while his fellow actor got to be exuberant. Perhaps aware that this might be difficult for Lane, Williams was exceptionally generous about his co-star, aware that it was he and not Nathan who would be expected to have everyone cracking up. 'Oh, it was really hard,' he said in an interview with *Reddit*, when asked if he was tempted to laugh. 'His voice, that character, Agador

Spartacus. It wasn't just me that had a hard time. [Director] Mike Nichols would laugh so hard they would have to put a blanket over his head. The other guy who was so funny was Gene Hackman. His speech about the leaves in New England was one of the funniest, driest pieces of comedy I'd ever seen.'

The movie garnered generally good reviews and praise from the Gay & Lesbian Alliance Against Defamation for 'going beyond the stereotypes to see the character's depth and humanity. The film celebrates differences and points out the outrageousness of hiding those differences'. Perhaps most importantly of all, in the eyes of Hollywood at least, it made a huge amount of money too. It proved that Williams, in a gay role, could also be the straight man.

In actual fact, he had first been approached to play the drag role. He had also been asked to drag up the previous year in Julie Newmar's *To Wong Foo, Thanks For Everything!* (1995) but refused both parts for the same reason: having already dressed as a woman in *Mrs. Doubtfire*, he didn't want to get typecast. 'My manager begged me to play Albert,' he explained. 'He said it would give me carte blanche to be the most outrageous I've ever been. But I've been a big bad woman before. The challenge for me was to play the more subtle Armand and see if I could still get my share of laughs. It's bad enough that the *Mrs. Doubtfire* people want to put me back in drag for a sequel. I don't have to wiggle into a bra and pantyhose for every other studio in Hollywood.'

The never-to-be-realised sequel to *Mrs. Doubtfire* was, indeed, already under discussion but, even at that point, it was clear that the filmmakers were experiencing difficulties in coming up with a decent script.

In contrast to his extraordinary professional output, Williams was going through a calmer stage in his personal life. Most youngsters want their parents to put on silly voices when they read them a story but Robin's children were the opposite, telling him to calm down. Interviewers began to comment on the fact that he didn't tend to go off into funny voices in the middle of interviews as much as previously, which was surely a good sign. Apart from anything else, he was a father now, three times over and, as such, was required by his children to act as a grown-up. He and Marsha were working very much as a team, managing his career and their charitable work, not to mention their home life. And as one of the most bankable stars in the world, the offers continued to flood in. Life was good.

On screen, however, he was manic as ever and again invited comparisons to a classic 1988 film – *Big*, in which Tom Hanks plays a twelve-year-old in the body of a grown man – when he starred in *Jack* (1996), in which he played a ten-year-old in the body of a grown man. In *Big*, the mix-up came about because of a mysterious fortune-teller machine, while in *Jack*, it was because of a premature ageing condition but there were certainly similarities, not least because both had to deal with the awkward subject of girls.

Robin was initially reluctant to take on the project. 'When the script for *Jack* came to me, I gave it a resounding no,' he told the *Calgary Sun*. 'I told Disney I'd been there and done that enough. I'm 44 and furry. The only thing I'm really suited for is the musical version of *Congo*. [But] Disney pulled out the big guns. They called my friend Francis Ford Coppola to direct and he assured me I'd never played this kind of character before.'

Francis Ford Coppola is certainly a name to deal with. Robin signed on the dotted line and proceeded to spend a couple of weeks bonding with the child actors who were to play Jack's friends, camping, playing baseball and telling ghost stories. 'It was like *Lord Of The Flies* day-care centre,' he said.

'I came up with this concept to have Robin in a situation with eight or nine nine-year-olds,' Coppola told the *Toronto Sun* in 1996. 'I'm an old camp counselor and we did all sorts of activities. We made peanut butter and jelly sandwiches and slept on the mountain.'

'We called it Camp Coppola,' added Robin. 'We did kid things, rode bikes for days, went to toy stores. By the end, it was weird, I'd assimilated all this stuff. It was like time travelling by association. Y'know, it's all little things at that age that are important – your "stuff," things they have, friendships. When the world collapses, it collapses completely. That's why they break down and cry and the next minute feel great.'

Coppola was fulsome in his praise: Williams was

'childlike but not childish or even remotely a child. His inventiveness and enthusiasm are what make Robin seem so childlike,' he said and both of them took the project so seriously that they got a ten-year-old boy on board to help him prepare for the role. 'Robin would go through each scene first,' explained Coppola. 'Then his adviser would do it independently with Robin watching. There were things the boy would do that would absolutely amaze Robin and he would adjust what he was doing.'

The two men felt the film reflected a sadness in their own childhoods. 'I lived in that big house and I was pretty much alone,' Robin told the *Toronto Sun*, in a sober tone that would quite often emerge from all the humour. 'I still went to school, but I was kind of out in a big farm in the country way away from everybody. I remember getting picked on, having to find alternate ways to get home 'cause you don't want to get your ass kicked. I was picked on for being small. At a certain point I felt fat, pudgy. That's why I became a wrestler in high school. At least if you're only going to be 103 pounds, you can kick another 103-pound guy's ass.'

It seemed Coppola didn't have much fun as a child either. 'I think it was Hemingway who said that to be a great artist you have to have an unhappy childhood,' he said. 'I had polio as a child and was kept from any contact with kids. There was a lot of longing. And I think that was why I empathized with this film.

'I read the script of *Jack* with Robin in mind. And I read

it kind of like Kafka's *Metamorphosis*. I said, "If you accept him as a giant cockroach, it's going to be good. If you don't accept Robin as a 10-year-old, the premise falls.'"

But the audience *did* accept Robin as a kid – they had already done so in many of his previous roles, whether or not he'd been playing a child. But Williams was, by now, halfway through his forties, married with children and a serious A-lister. He had, beyond a doubt, grown up.

Miranda: *What happened?*
Mrs. Doubtfire: *He was quite fond of the drink. It was the drink that killed him.*
Miranda: *How awful. He was an alcoholic?*
Mrs. Doubtfire: *No, he was hit by a Guinness truck. So it was quite literally the drink that killed him.*

MRS. DOUBTFIRE (1993)

CHAPTER TEN

PICASSOS AND PRINCES

'The only reason Mickey Mouse has four
fingers is because he can't pick up a cheque.'
ROBIN WILLIAMS, ON HIS FINANCIAL DISPUTE WITH DISNEY

It didn't take long for matters with Disney to calm down:
to be fair, it made no sense for either party if a major star
and a major film company continued to indulge in a feud.
And anyway, they wanted Williams to work for them again.
Robin addressed this in typically knockabout style.

'No, I don't have a contract with Disney,' he told the
Toronto Sun. 'Actually, they have a contract on me. A man
named Tony has been following me around. [Mafioso
voice]: "I want you to stop saying things about Mr. Eisner.
The man has the warmth of a snow pea." "You made fun
of the King!" "Robin, we'd like to talk to you outside."

'Merchandising tie-ins, the whole thing. I don't mind if they make dolls,' he continued. 'It's when they use my voice that it gets interesting.' But that Picasso had clearly helped, although Robin's version of events was a little different. 'The thing is they didn't give me a Picasso as a payback for violating the agreement,' he continued. 'The Picasso came first, then they violated the agreement, then we broke off the marriage. Then they apologized, and that was all I wanted. I wanted them to say, "We violated the agreement and then we put out a press campaign that made it look as if you were sticking us up for money." Studios do this all the time, but they just don't cop to it. "Shhh! You mean lie?" But they did and they admitted it and now we're back. It was tough for a while. How do you tell the kids, "Daddy's fighting with Disney, so we won't be going to Orlando for a while? No more plush toys or Hunchback packs or merchandising."'

Williams, incidentally, had been paid $75,000 for a film that took over $600 million at the box office but that wasn't the issue: the principle was at stake.

But everyone had kissed and made up, just in time to make an Aladdin sequel, *Aladdin and the King of Thieves* (1996). This was not, in fact, the first sequel – that had been *The Return of Jafar* (1994), with the Blue Genie voiced by Dan Castellaneta (Homer Simpson), when feelings were still running high – and it was being made for the video market rather than the cinema but it was in everyone's interests to get Williams back on board. In fact, some of the film had already been made using Castellaneta again, with a third of the animation done but, when Robin signed up, everyone was happy to start again from scratch.

'With Robin, it's a much stronger film,' Ann Daly, president of Buena Vista Home Video, told *TV Guide* in 1996. 'It elevates the project to a new level. Nobody can do what he does in the recording studio. The animators were inspired by him.' (It seemed a little unfair on Castellaneta but that's showbiz.)

In 1997 Williams put in the performance that finally got him an Oscar in *Good Will Hunting*, the film that also launched the careers of Matt Damon and, to a lesser extent, Ben Affleck (who had already begun to make his mark), although the award was for Best Supporting Actor rather than as the lead role. The story, written by Affleck and Damon, starred Damon in the lead: it involved Will Hunting, a mathematical genius who is a blue-collar worker. After his gifts come to light, he almost ends up in jail for assaulting a police officer but is let off if he agrees to study mathematics with a famous professor (Stellan Skarsgård) and sees a therapist, Sean Maguire (Williams), who also had to deal with many issues in his past. Will is then able to reassess his life and starts to make something of himself.

The film was a massive success – one of the biggest of Williams' career – grossing over $225 million during its theatrical run and earning nine Oscar nominations. Along with Robin's win, Affleck and Damon got an Oscar for the

Best Original Screenplay. It was one of those films both beloved of audiences and critics alike.

'Damon and Affleck were smart enough to realise that they wouldn't get their script filmed just by writing good parts for themselves,' wrote Quentin Curtis in 1998 in the *Daily Telegraph*. 'They needed a major star, and so they dangled the prospect of a great supporting role before the A-list names. The part is that of Will's psychiatrist, whose own life has gone off the rails, and who goads Will into maturity. Robin Williams took the bait, and he gets to deliver two speeches so juicy they look set to become actors' audition pieces: one about the virtue of imperfection, the other a hostile lecture to Will on the difference between knowledge and experience.'

'The strength of *Good Will Hunting* lies in the amazing assurance of its script, and the backing both its cast and makers give it,' said *Empireonline*. 'Director Van Sant steers well clear of unnecessary sentiment, opting instead to find the emotional reality and harshness within the story. Damon is superb, his pal Affleck equally strong. But, in a movie that exudes quality, however, it is Robin Williams that provides both its heart and its highlight – the Oscar, in this case, was entirely deserved.'

'Mr. Williams is wonderfully strong and substantial here; Mr. Damon, very much the supernova, is mercurial in ways that keep his character steadily surprising,' wrote Janet Maslin in *The New York Times*. 'The screenplay's best moments come in a couple of long, defining monologues (particularly one from Sean in the Boston Public Gardens) that angrily bring Will and Sean to life.'

'A towering performance by Matt Damon in the lead, and a superlative ensemble headed by a terrific Robin Williams, elevate *Good Will Hunting*, Gus Van Sant's emotionally involving psychological drama, a notch or two above the mainstream therapeutic sensibility of its story,' wrote Emanuel Levy in *Variety*. 'Centering on a brilliant working-class youngster who's forced to come to terms with his creative genius and true feelings, this beautifully realized tale is always engaging and often quite touching.' The film has, to date at least, survived the test of time: it is now considered one of the finest of its era and Damon and Affleck went on to become massive stars.

For his part, Williams was thrilled. 'A lot of people are coming to me, thanking me for *Good Will Hunting*, because it touched them so much,' he said. 'That's just as meaningful to me as someone saying "I laughed my ass off, cuz, y'know, you're one funny bastard."' His role in the film, people's reaction to it and the Oscar all brought him a sense of validation – that at last he was truly being recognised as a serious actor.

Indeed, he was becoming an increasingly serious figure. He was still doing a great deal to support Christopher Reeve, accompanying him to Puerto Rico to attend an American Paralysis Association benefit and appearing increasingly reluctant to indulge interviewers with his zany side. 'It's too early,' he complained to one, adding, 'I just want to work with characters, with great ensembles of people.' He was, in fact, doing just that: appearing as Osric in Kenneth Branagh's *Hamlet* (1996), the tragic story of the Prince of Denmark, and as a malevolent bomb-making chemist in *The Secret Agent* (1996), based on Joseph Conrad's novel. His billing on *Hamlet* was well below the usual, in the midst of a very starry ensemble indeed. Even the bit parts were played by superstars, with Billy Crystal (another funnyman who wanted to be serious) as First Gravedigger, Judi Dench as Hecuba, Julie Christie (Gertrude), Derek Jacobi (Claudius), Kate Winslet (Ophelia) and even Gérard Depardieu putting in an appearance as Reynaldo. Jack Lemmon played Marcellus. It was, to put it mildly, an eclectic cast.

But Robin was happy for a lowlier billing (although being a part of that crowd spoke volumes in itself) because, to put it bluntly, the pressure was off. When your name is above the billing, your neck is also on the line: if the film fails, it will be seen to have been because of you. Williams had had a fair number of flops in his time (one interviewer commented on the fact that, although he was prepared to admit this, it was noticeable that he never talked about *Popeye* anymore) but, in cases like this, life was a little easier. He did not have to carry the film.

For he had discovered that enormous success also brings with it enormous pressure; he had his detractors and there was no shortage of volunteers willing to throw mud if something went wrong. Five of his films in the 1990s

– *The Birdcage, Jumanji, Mrs. Doubtfire, Aladdin* and *Hook* – had grossed more than $100 million and that brought about pressures all of their own. He was still turning up unannounced at comedy clubs – 'cheaper than therapy' – but equally, he now wanted to be seen as an *homme sérieuse*. To further emphasise his unusual position – and as an added source of pressure – he had been called the 'funniest man alive' by both *People* and *Vogue*, which inevitably led to some being at pains to say they didn't find him that funny.

'They should have just pinned a sign on my butt saying "Kick me,"' said Robin. Quite simply, he couldn't win.

And for an *homme sérieuse*, it must be said that he made some pretty ropey film choices. There was *Fathers' Day* (1997) with Billy Crystal, in which the two actors played men who were both convinced they were the father of the same boy, with the mother (Nastassja Kinski) lying to both in order to get them to help find her son.

'Billy and I have been looking for a project to do together for years. We work so well off each other on the Comedy Relief specials that it seemed a natural screen pairing,' said Robin. 'Whenever we're on stage or in front of a camera together, it's like two elk spraying musk. It's a healthy competition. It keeps our comedy antlers sharp. Every comic is competitive. To deny that is to deny the essence of comedy.'

The essence of comedy was not, alas, evident in the film either, which pretty much sank without trace.

He had a rather happier experience with *What Dreams May Come* (1998) – a reference to Hamlet's 'To be or not to be' soliloquy – in which he co-starred with Cuba Gooding Jr. This was an extraordinary film, almost metaphysical in its intent, in which Williams and Annabella Sciorra play Chris and Annie, a married couple who lose both of their children in a car crash before Chris, too, dies in another car accident. He ascends to Heaven, where he is able in some way to communicate with Annie until, consumed by despair, she kills herself. She is thus consigned to Hell and Chris, despite many warnings to the contrary, descends to rescue her. Initially, he chooses to stay in Hell with her but, in a desire to save him, Annie is knocked out of her despair and the two are able to once more ascend to Heaven. They are reunited with their children before being reincarnated to meet on Earth once again.

The film looked spectacular: it posited the theory that a person's vision of Heaven or Hell is defined by a character's subconscious and, as Annie was an artist with a profound influence on Chris, Heaven is spectacular. On the other hand, Hell is so horrible that some critics felt the need to warn viewers in advance.

Quite a plot and, if Robin wanted to be taken seriously, this was the right way to go about it. Roger Ebert, of the *Chicago Sun-Times* and not always a Williams fan, was full of praise: 'This is a film that even in its imperfect form shows how movies can imagine the unknown, can lead our imaginations into wonderful places. And it contains heartbreakingly effective performances by Robin Williams and Annabella Sciorra,' he said.

But Stephen Holden, writing in *The New York Times*, didn't like it one bit. 'It wasn't so long ago that love, in Hollywood-speak, was supposed to mean never having to say you're sorry,' he wrote. '*What Dreams May Come*, one of the most elaborate metaphysical love stories ever tackled by Hollywood, lays out a whole new set of irritating catchphrases to define the quest for a love that triumphs over death. These range from the blunt "Never give up," which is repeated like a mantra throughout the movie, to portentous utterances about winning when you lose and losing when you win.' Particular bile was reserved for Robin: 'Robin Williams, with his Humpty Dumpty grin and crinkly moist eyes dripping with empathy.'

James Berardinelli of *Reelviews* was complimentary though. 'Many movies have offered representations of heaven and hell, but few with as much conviction and creativity as *What Dreams May Come*,' he wrote. 'The plot, which focuses on the sacrifices one man will make for true love, is neither complicated nor original, but, bolstered by the director's incredible visual sense, it becomes an affecting piece of drama.'

Meanwhile, Owen Gleiberman of *Entertainment Weekly* said, 'There's a central contradiction in a fairy tale like this one: the film may preach to the audience about matters of the spirit, but its bejeweled special-effects vision of the afterlife can't help but come off as aggressively literal-minded.'

But, while the critics' reaction may have been mixed, the public loved it and so, too, did the film industry, awarding it an Oscar for Best Visual Effects and an Art Directors Guild Award for Excellence in Production Design.

'You feel a lot,' Robin admitted to the *Toronto Sun*, very much not in comic mode not only for his performance in the film but for the accompanying interviews too. 'There are a lot of emotions, and you think: "Do I want to go through this?" That's the main question. In the end, I decided, "Yes!" But it's hard stuff to deal with, all the loss and all the pain of it all. There were only a couple of days where you got to go: "This is a good day." Even in the moments when he was in heaven, he was still dealing with not wanting to let go and trying to connect with her [his wife]. It's hard when you read it and you think: "Do I want to go there, to go to those places?" But what is extraordinary is the vision of a very subjective heaven and hell.'

Some of the film was shot in Marin County, near Williams' home and so at least he was able to return to his family every night, which kept some of the demons at bay. 'It deals with such emotionally intense issues, I didn't know if I'd want to do this for four or five months, be near this kind of dark pain and loss that are at the core of it,' he told *CNN*. 'But as we kept doing it, I thought, "Well, it's certainly interesting." And it makes you look at your own life and how you live your life – but that's a side effect of being near this kind of intense emotion.'

When he wasn't having to access inner turmoil, however,

Robin was fairly happy, not least because, finally, he now had an Oscar in the bag. 'It's nice to have, like Bertolt Brecht said, a passport to go anywhere,' he admitted to *CNN*. 'It's nice to have that option, to have that kind of opportunity where people say, "You can try this, because you've proven you can do a character, a full-out character, a character who has this emotional range." That allows you just more opportunities to have the comedic, which is wonderful, and to have these dramatic roles. It just gives you a larger range, a bigger field to play on.'

However, it had been obvious for some time now that Williams was as much a serious actor as he was a comedian – 'I go both ways' – and his output continued to be phenomenal. There was a turn in a somewhat sour Woody Allen number, *Deconstructing Harry* (1997), a return to clowning in *Flubber* (1997), in which he played an absent-minded professor and another serious bout in *Jakob the Liar* (1999), about Polish Jews in World War II (Robin himself was frequently and mistakenly assumed to be Jewish).

Marsha remained heavily involved in every aspect of his life and this is one of the films she worked particularly closely on. Jakob was a former restaurant owner living in a Polish ghetto; his neighbours mistakenly believe he has a radio and Jakob starts to give them hope by pretending to hear news flashes. Eventually, the Nazis hear about this inmate with a radio and go after him. The film ends tragically, as it was bound to do given the tale it told. Written and directed by the Hungarian filmmaker Peter Kassovitz, it was originally intended to be a French production but the sensitivity of the subject matter put the French producers off.

'I then decided to rewrite the screenplay in English and tailor it for Robin Williams,' Kassovitz told the *Calgary Sun* in an interview that made it clear that the actor was more reliant on Marsha than ever. 'You can't go directly to Robin. You have to go through agents and lawyers to get to Marsha and then she decides if Robin gets to see the material. Robin relies a great deal on Marsha and she has a great deal of power because she has Robin and people want him in their movies.'

'I met with Peter after I read the script and we worked on it for about a year before I gave it to Robin. This is not a unique situation,' said Marsha in 1999 to the *Calgary Sun*. 'I worked on *Mrs. Doubtfire* for a year before Robin ever saw the script. I look for characters I don't think he has done before. Much of what producers and writers want Robin to do is stuff he's already done. [I treat him] like any other actor. I wouldn't think of giving an actor a screenplay until it was pretty much at production level.'

As for Robin, he was perfectly happy with this arrangement, realising that he could rely on his wife and that, unlike so many of the Hollywood players he encountered, she would give him her honest opinion. 'She is the only person who is brutally honest with me,' he said. 'Most people would prefer to tell me what they think I want to hear. Not Marsha. She refuses to let me recycle old schtick just because it works. It's vital to have someone who is determined to see that I grow as an actor.'

Looking back at their obvious closeness at that stage and how well they worked as a team, the couple's subsequent divorce seems all the more tragic. But for all that Robin was at that point holding it together, staying away from the drugs and the booze and getting into cycling, he was alas to go seriously off the rails once more.

Next, however, in what it must be said some people considered the nadir of his career, there was *Patch Adams* (1998), which was about the last film to help him grow as an actor. It is obvious, in retrospect, why the project might have seemed like a good idea at the time: it was based on the true story of Dr Hunter 'Patch' Adams, a doctor with some very unconventional views about how to treat patients. It was set in the 1990s, when Patch was nearly expelled from Virginia Medical School for 'excessive happiness'. Unfortunately, to the impartial observer, this reveals the film's weaknesses at a glance.

Patch believes that humour should be used to treat patients but that humour includes dressing up as a clown and setting up a giant pair of legs at an obstetrics conference and, while people can be good at being a doctor or good at being a clown, not many of them embrace both these fields. Humour can be tasteless and, alas, not even funny.

The critics hated it and so, too, did the original Patch

Adams, who not only attacked the film but also slammed Williams, although he later withdrew some of his remarks. But star power is star power. The movie still made over $200 million worldwide, with various Oscar and Golden Globe nominations (none of them won).

But no one involved saw the critical reaction coming, least of all Robin, who gave his usual series of cheerful interviews to publicise the film. 'His critics call him a modern Don Quixote who's deluded, but Patch is not chasing windmills,' he told the *Calgary Sun*. 'He's committed, dedicated and intelligent and he does everything possible to help his patients.'

In one scene, the doctor entertained cancer patients: 'Most of the children in that scene really are cancer patients,' revealed Robin. 'They got their roles in the movie through the Make-A-Wish Foundation. Their reactions are spontaneous. It's not acting.' He also met the real Patch, adding, 'We became instant friends. He made me laugh so much it hurt. He's an outrageous guy, an absolute born clown.' It must have hurt him a great deal when his new friend was extremely critical of him after the film's release. But that's showbiz, them's the breaks.

In another interview, this time with the *Toronto Sun*, Robin actually, without realising it, put his finger on another of the trouble points in the movie. 'We do Patch's time in medical school,' he said. 'It's kind of like the beginning of this outrageous character. Patch was very uplifting. We try to show that. But we also show that he could be irritating, too, with his desire to always challenge the system.' There is, of course, a danger in portraying someone irritating onscreen – it can come across as irritating.

Williams was now facing another problem: fans, especially those from the early days, were beginning to complain that they wanted him to be funny again in the way he used to be. In fact, he never stopped being funny – the ongoing appearances in comedy clubs confirmed that, as did his frequent appearances on talk shows, where he seemed to think it was his duty to have people almost weeping with laughter from the moment he went on. But Robin was the clown who wanted to play Hamlet – more than that, he was the clown who could play Hamlet, or Osric, at least. And this was something that he would never entirely resolve: comedian or serious actor? And why couldn't people accept he was both?

'People just want to be entertained,' he told one interviewer. 'They see you do something wonderful and they want you to do it again... and again... and again... until they get tired of it and want somebody else. That's the danger. If you do it again and again and again, they'll finally go, "Harrumph! Seen that!" But that's what you wanted! "Used to..." And you're dead.'

One particular incident with a fan seems to have upset him. 'It's the woman coming up to me in the airport and going: "Be zany! Be zany!" What? She wants me to be wild. So you have to keep re-inventing yourself like Madonna. This year is her Indian year. Last year was the Valkyrie year.

Two years ago it was the Edsel-tit year. What do you do? You change yourself.

'I've been freed because films such as *Dead Poets Society* or *Awakenings* or *The Fisher King* or *Good Will Hunting* have been successful. And it isn't just the Academy Award. That perception started a while ago. I re-invented myself from comedy to do drama. You keep changing. So it's just another colour you get to paint with.'

But the frustration was palpable. Robin could see that he could veer between the two different disciplines, so why couldn't anyone else see the same?

> Will: *Do you like apples?*
> Clark: *Yeah.*
> Will: *Well, I got her number. How do you*
> *like them apples?*
> GOOD WILL HUNTING (1997)

CHAPTER ELEVEN

GAME
BOY

*'Cocaine is God's way of saying you're
making too much money.'*
ROBIN WILLIAMS

When you break free of one addiction, usually you end up
with another. That's the received wisdom and it tends to be
right. That had happened to Robin: when he gave up drink
and drugs in the early 1980s, he took up cycling and, in a
hilly area like San Francisco, he had the perfect landscape
in which to become as good as any pro. And so he was. He
built up a large cycle collection and anyone who cycled
with him quickly came to see that this was not a man to be
trifled with. Besides, it was good for him: physical exercise
helps anyone with depression and the more he cycled, the
better he felt.

He was friends with the cyclist Lance Armstrong (this was before the disgraceful revelations about Armstrong's drug-taking) and would cross the Atlantic to see him in the Tour de France. 'I love it over there,' he told *Sports Illustrated* in 2003. 'I love to watch his teammates, the domestiques. These guys go flat-out for whatever Lance needs – food, water, pull him up a hill, radio's broken, whatever. They're all hunched over on their bikes, bringing him things. It's like, "Quasimodo is Gunga Din!" The coach says, "Hey, would you mind coming back to the van and getting a water for Lance?" And the guy has to drop all the way back, get the water, bust his hump all the way back to the front and hand him the water. And then Lance goes, "This one's too warm." Turns out domestique is French for slave!'

He also cherished his bike collection. 'You can get them for six or $7,000,' he told *Autograph* magazine. 'They're cheaper than Maseratis and easier to store. They're all hanging in the garage. I love riding them. A lot of them are hand-made sculptures, really. Most of them are made by craftsmen.'

Tony Tom was the owner of a San Francisco bicycle store and Robin's biking partner. 'He just loved cycling – it was his outlet,' Tony told *Nightline* in an emotional interview after Williams' death, during which he was clearly on the edge of tears. 'He came [to the shop] shortly after John Belushi passed away from a drug overdose. He needed some kind of an outlet and said, "I'll tell ya – cycling saved my life." And he said, "Biking is a whole lot better for you than cocaine." He just loved cycling. [The area around San Francisco] to him was his backyard, so to speak, he loved getting out.

'I'd see him probably once a week when he was around. He was a very avid rider and a very proficient rider. And he was always cordial. I can't remember him refusing ever to sign an autograph, or not talking to anyone who just walked up to him. He'd always respond. He was incredibly gracious and very giving. He was a really good man. We're all going to miss him and I think we should cherish the gifts that he's left us, all those performances, all those movies. There's never going to be another guy like that.'

Indeed not. But Williams had developed another addiction too: one that was nothing like as good for him and, in all probability, actually the opposite. It had been known that he was a keen gamer – both Zelda and his son Cody had been named after video games, the latter after Final Fight – but it wasn't until the early years of the twenty-first century that anyone outside of his close circle of intimates knew just how far it really went.

Not that Robin was trying to hide it: he was quite open about his pastime. In fact, he was something of an Internet junkie, not just gaming but venturing into chat rooms (not necessarily revealing his identity, although rumours that he sometimes posed as a six-year-old girl called Samantha were not true) and having fun online.

'I'm not afraid of it, I'm actually kind of addicted to it,' he admitted in an interview with *Zap2it* in the early noughties, that is, before widespread Wi-Fi. Indeed, his computer had become his regular travelling companion, which, while standard today, was less so in the days before smartphones and iPads. It tended mainly to be people travelling on businesses who took their computers everywhere. 'When I find out a hotel doesn't have a DSL [digital subscriber loop], it's like "What? There's no toilet?" Once you get used to high speed you ain't going back,' he declared. 'Once you've had DSL, you don't go back. I play games, I'm not going to lie about it, and when you play online against someone else, it's the best. Especially when you're playing against a 12-year-old kid who's been playing the game for a year and knows all the secrets. I'm fascinated by military games.'

Did he look at his own fan sites? 'That's like bobbing for razors, that's really bad news because you'll find great things and horrible things. I did it once,' he revealed. 'You'll find people who love what you're doing and people who despise what you're doing. That's the Web, that's the gamut of all personalities.' Of course, this was before Facebook, Twitter, Instagram and trolling; a period when the full range of opportunities offered by the Internet were still unknown.

But Robin did love his games. He was an aficionado of First Person Shooter, Half-Life and War Craft 3: 'There are a million games and there are mods with these games,' he said, displaying some in-depth knowledge of the area. 'The mods are taking these games and basically redesigning it and doing it on their own thing. There's a game called Half-Life and these guys made up a total different take on it using the engine to make a World War II engine called Day of Defeat with Germans and Americans doing kind of like a Normandy beach type thing. But these guys made it on their own and the company basically kind of gave them their blessing. It's amazing. It's a world. It has its own mythology, plus clans and groups.'

In fact, it turned out that Robin knew a huge amount about it. 'They start off with a kind of primitive version where people were off wandering around conducting quests but now with Morrow Wind and Never Winter at Night and Dark Age of Camelot, people are in there creating characters and building up the characters to the point where if they build up a character with enough points they'll sell it on eBay,' he added. And then, the potential downside appeared to occur to him: 'Just as long as it doesn't become like... Well, because it's video cocaine, it can be as addictive as anything in this world with computer widows. You have to limit it though because it's addictive because of this world. I guess the worst-case scenario was some kid who killed himself because his character died. You have to go, "Wait a minute. This has gone way beyond the limits of a game."'

One of Williams' tragedies was that, although an exceptionally intelligent man, he couldn't see the truth about himself. Not only was it staring him in the face but he'd even identified the danger: it was addictive. And while there was relatively little downside in being addicted to cycling, an obsession with gaming was something else altogether, especially for someone who struggled with depression. Alone, in a room with his computer and his thoughts, was the worst possible scenario for him to be dealing with and, in the wake of his death, there was some speculation that this obsessive gaming had played havoc with his state of mind.

But, as is so often the case, no one saw any potential concerns. Robin appeared for a stint on *The Tonight Show Starring Jimmy Fallon* and talked about how much he loved Call of Duty; he loved role-playing too (perhaps unsurprisingly for an actor). After his death, it was announced that he was to be memorialised in World of Warcraft. This was a side to him that his fans didn't see so much but it was very much there. He performed live at Google's keynote session at the 2006 Consumer Electronics Show and participated in a live demonstration of Spore at the invitation of the game's creator, Will Wright, at the 2006 Electronic Entertainment Expo, in which players created basic, spore-like creatures, which evolved into small communities, then cities, countries, planets and outer space.

Williams created something that was flexible in the extreme – 'This is a creature that can kiss its own butt' – and ended up with three sets of arms, a thin torso and short legs. 'I'm putting together a creature that would make Darwin say, "Hey, I'm not taking acid ever again,"' he said. And he gave it a very long nose. 'This is basically a creature that can do coke a mile away.' He followed this up by being one of a number of celebrities to participate in the 2007 Worldwide Dungeons & Dragons Game Day in London.

In his online interview with *Reddit*, he talked about it: 'I'm still waiting for the next Call of Duty,' he said. 'It's been very unusual for me because I've done trips overseas to Iraq and Afghanistan, and I would see guys who had just come back from patrol playing Call of Duty, and I would say "You're living this stuff! And yet you're still playing this game..."'

But again, there was that note of caution: 'I'm playing a game called Battlestation Pacific,' he continued. 'I'm looking forward to the next Xbox. I can't imagine the graphics being any better. It will be like these characters are living in your house. I'll have to be doing duck and cover just to get to the bathroom! For the WiiU or the PS4, at this point I haven't seen them yet but I might have to check into the cyber wing at Betty Ford.'

And again, 'It's like cyber-cocaine,' he told the *Daily Telegraph* in a 2011 interview. 'Especially if you're online playing against other people, it's totally addictive, you get lost in the world.' That was half of the appeal, of course – there was nothing he wanted more than to lose himself and, if he couldn't do that with the consciousness-altering stimulants of alcohol and drugs, he would find something else instead.

This resulted in some very strange postings. Someone calling themselves DigInTheCrates started a thread on an entertainment site called *The Vesti* under the heading 'Are people bracing themselves for the fact that Robin Williams will die soon?' This was all very well but it was posted on 8 August 2014, three days before Williams' death. Not that anyone knew that, of course.

'Are you going to kill him or something?' was one reply.

DigInTheCrates said, 'He's old and his health is poor which is why I made this thread. no I don't plan to kill him you sick weirdos, why would I kill someone I love.'

And then, of course, poor Robin did die, prompting an explosion of action on the thread, mainly (but not seriously) blaming DigInTheCrates.

'Yep op is possessed by Satan.'

'Police gonna see this thread.'

'did anyone else think "I really hope RW didn't find this thread, see we haven't been entertained in well over 10 yrs and end it all."'

'OP is the angel of death.'

'Don't blame me,' insisted DigInTheCrates. 'I blame all you people for not loving and appreciating him enough while he was here.'

But they were not slow to honour him once he was gone. In the aftermath of his death, it was not only fellow actors who paid tributes but fellow gamers too. A user called Vulpes wrote on a *Zeldauniverse.net* forum, 'Considering his connection to "Zelda," does anyone think the community sending his family some kind of organized condolences or something like that would be appropriate? We could raise money for his Windfall charity, maybe?' Many others chimed in with praise: for all that Robin felt like an outsider for so much of his life, he was certainly accepted here. His fellow gamers loved him: by going public about his hobby, he had shown himself to be one of them.

Vulpes subsequently told *Salon.com*, 'The most impressive thing about Williams' relationship with gaming was how shameless he was about it. These days, if a celebrity admits to playing games, it's frequently treated as a dirty secret: "I know it's nerdy, but I play video games!"'

But it couldn't have been good for his health. Some years ago, Dr Douglas Gentile of Iowa State University took part in a survey called 'Pathological Video Game Use Among Youths: A Two-Year Longitudinal Study', which was published in *Pediatrics*. Of course, Williams wasn't a youth but, reading what Dr. Gentile had to say in an interview about his study, it is hard not to suspect that the conclusions applied to him too.

'I was expecting to find that the depression led to gaming,' he said. 'But we found the opposite in that study. The depression seemed to follow the gaming. As kids became addicted – if you want to use that word – then their depression seemed to get worse. And, as they stopped being addicted, the depression seemed to lift. I was expecting to find that the depression led to gaming. But we found the opposite in that study.'

He came to believe, however, that, in actual fact, the two went hand in hand. 'I don't really think [the depression] is following,' he said. 'I think it's truly comorbid [when two medical conditions are intertwined]. When a person gets one disorder, they often get more. If you've been diagnosed with bipolar disorder, a year or two later you might end up with anxiety problems or social phobias. They all start interacting with each other and make each other worse. [The test subjects' gaming 'addiction' and mental health problems] are close enough in time that they're probably affecting each other. As you get more depressed you retreat more into games, which doesn't help, because it doesn't actually solve the problem. It doesn't help your depression, so your depression gets worse, so you play more games, so your depression gets worse, etc. It becomes a negative spiral.'

It certainly wasn't a healthy pastime for someone who had been suffering from mental-health problems all his life.

But in the meantime, the films and occasional television appearances went on. In 1997 Robin appeared with his friend Billy Crystal in an episode of *Friends* – 'The One With The Ultimate Fighting Champion' – and, as the new millennium approached, there were plenty of projects lined up. He played a robot in *Bicentennial Man* (1999), based on a novella by Isaac Asimov – one with feelings, natch, which was a thrill to a science-fiction fan like him: 'I read *I, Robot* in college,' he told *Science Fiction Weekly*. '*Bicentennial Man* I'd only read after we decided to do the movie. And then I read *The Positronic Man*, which is the book that Asimov wrote with Robert Silverberg. It's pretty interesting, because [the movie] keeps to the spirit of what he was capturing with robots. It's weird that Asimov has never been made into a movie before; I'm pretty sure that's correct.

'It talks about artificial intelligence and human behavior. I've always been fascinated by both. Hence acting. That's kind of the drill, really, I mean, to find different aspects of it. But with this, it's the idea of a creature evolving. And Asimov was basically talking about a moral, humane creature, of robots as being these sentient beings who were bound by the three laws like commandments. They can't violate them, even if they wanted to.'

In the event, the film got fairly mixed reviews and failed to set the house on fire.

One of Williams' most appealing characteristics was his vulnerability: unusually for someone who had been bullied as a child, he was not afraid to tell people when he was hurt. And the reviews he'd been getting recently really did hurt. He was never able to escape the charge of sentimentality – sometimes deservedly, as with the mawkish *Patch Adams* – but that didn't mean he could just laugh it off.

'Oh God, it was frightening,' he told *totaldvd.net* in a 2002 interview. 'I'd read reviews about other movies and they would attack me again. One woman said the film she was reviewing was so bad the director should be put on a desert island with the people that made *Patch Adams* and may they all drown with Robin Williams. I was like, "Oh lady, come on, you don't have to beat me up again." I think these last few movies have changed people's perception a bit, though.'

He was referring to a trio in which he played a number of very creepy characters indeed. In *One Hour Photo* (2002) he plays a lonely photo-lab technician who becomes obsessed to the point of stalking the Yorkin family, whose pictures he develops. *Death To Smoochy* (2002), the second film, was a dark comedy about a children's entertainer wreaking horrible revenge on a rival and then there was the massively underrated *Insomnia* (also 2002), in which he starred with Al Pacino. The film was centred around Pacino's character, a Los Angeles cop sent with his partner to Alaska, who unwittingly kills said partner and gets drawn into a very unhealthy web. Robin was quite superb as a truly flesh-crawling killer who enters into a phone relationship with Pacino, in which he admits his guilt.

The film was both a commercial and critical success, so it cannot be said that Williams received the same kind of brickbats as he had from other films but it should have garnered even more praise than it did. It is entirely possible that his reputation was actively working against him with this one, to the extent that people couldn't quite believe that he was holding his own against the great Al Pacino – but he was.

Was this a deliberate move on his part, to play monsters after the cloying Patch? 'Ah yes, the brown period,' he told *totaldvd.net*. 'I didn't consciously go after darker movies, things just kind of happened that way in a weird synchronicity – first *One Hour Photo*, then *Death to Smoochy*, then *Insomnia*. They were so good and so strange, I thought,

I have to do these, especially with these directors attached. I saw [*Insomnia* director Chris Nolan's] *Memento* with twelve people and they were all like "What was that? I have to get a tattoo now: See Movie Again.'"

Robin was rather enjoying playing villains – and it was certainly casting him against type – but he was all too aware that there was the danger of getting typecast there too. 'If another nasty character comes along I'll probably do it, but if I keep on taking these roles it'll be like, "Oh, I see you're doing another one of those characters Mr. Williams,'" he said. 'I love playing characters like this because you're no longer bound by the laws of likeability and the audience get a surprise attack. People think "Oh, it's that nice man, he wouldn't do anything awful." And then they realise... He's a prick!'

He was clearly desperate not to be typecast and it was, perhaps, this that led him to return to stand-up proper. Throughout his career he had continued to perform live at clubs but this was going back to the big time. In 1986 he became the first comedian ever to appear at New York's Metropolitan Opera House and now he returned to Broadway with a stand-up act that was to be the fourth to be broadcast on HBO – this time live.

As ever, he was alone, totally exposed and on stage for over two hours – a feat that required prodigious amounts of energy, especially to keep up a performance as manic as his. He was met with a rapturous reception: no matter how much people appreciated his performances as an actor, what they loved best was how he could make them laugh. Really, really laugh. Robin made jokes about everything and anything: President Bush, golf, the Scots, Canada ('Canada's like a loft apartment over a really great party'), pandas ('they anaesthetize a panda, which is kind of redundant'), terrorism, Keith Richards, Afghanistan, intimate piercings, Sir Winston Churchill, giving cigarettes to babies, Michael Jackson claiming racism ('I'm like, "Honey, you gotta pick a race first."'), Canadian snowboarding, Donald Rumsfeld, psychics, Coco the gorilla, naughty Catholic priests (he got a few boos for that one), cats, terrorism, boxing, the Swiss, Ted Kennedy, the Oscars, Martha Stewart, Mike Tyson, airport security, Gandhi, Charlton Heston on gun control, turning fifty, Viagra, Osama bin Laden, Genesis (the Bible, not the group) and much, much more.

It was an astonishing performance and one he did not only night after night, through twenty-six sell-out shows, but live on TV too. (There was actually a glitch on that live broadcast. According to the *IMDb* website, 'At the beginning of this show, the announcer said, "Ladies and gentlemen, please welcome Robin Williams!" about five seconds too early. (He was supposed to say it so that the end of the announcement would butt right up against the first drumbeat of the opening music.) It was the only show on the entire tour where that happened.'

The audience was regularly reduced to weeping with laughter and many fans were publicly calling on Williams to return to stand-up and give up the film career. (As if!)

He, meanwhile, was in his element, doing what he had always done best and, when the show came out on DVD, there was another rush of sales. In 2003 it won a Grammy Award for Best Spoken Word Album.

Williams was still the pro he had always been.

But, as ever, sadness lurked in the wings. Christopher Reeve was not getting any better – and never would – and Robin's mother had died in 2001. Asked what the saddest thing he had ever experienced was, he replied, 'A double bill. The death of my father and the death of my mother.' He was then asked what he would, if he could, change about his childhood. 'Having a brother, not a half-brother,' he said. That lonely little boy was still very much there, albeit now a man in his fifties.

Robin couldn't help but dwell on serious issues. When he was gaming or on stage, he didn't have to deal with reality but, back in the cold light of day, there was an awful lot to feel gloomy about. 'Just the insane violence all over the world; that makes me cry,' he told *Autograph* magazine. 'And it's unrelenting. I was performing in a club in New York and afterward there was a guy sitting down with an Iranian, a Palestinian and an Israeli, and they all acknowledged that they want peace but they don't know how to get to it. How do you create a Palestinian homeland when there's a large amount of Palestinians who want to obliterate Israel? How do you stop this insane cycle that just keeps going on and on?'

Of course, these were questions to which there was

no answer but Robin was asking himself a lot of similar ones. And all the cycling in the world couldn't blot out his melancholia, to which, ultimately, there would be no cure. Frequently, he said that he'd had enough of playing little boys trapped in an adult man's body but that, ultimately, is what he truly was.

In 1984 he had taken part in a television show called *Superstars and Their Moms* (check it out on YouTube) and the Robin that comes across there is totally different from the one seen by the outside world. Clearly, he absolutely adores his mother but, unlike in almost any other public exchange he'd had with anyone, it was clear that she was the one in control of the conversation, not him. There was a great deal of banter between the two of them and enormous affection too.

Finally, he had got the parental attention he needed in a big way… But he didn't have his mother anymore.

> *'No matter what people tell you, words
> and ideas can change the world.'*
> ROBIN WILLIAMS

CHAPTER TWELVE

DECLINE
AND FALL

*'My battles with addiction definitely shaped how I am now.
They really made me deeply appreciate human contact. And
the value of friends and family, how precious that is.'*
ROBIN WILLIAMS

In retrospect, it is now quite clear that 2004 was the year
that marked the beginning of Williams' lengthy decline.
A once rock-solid marriage was to end, booze and rehab
beckoned and an extremely sad end awaited him. But there
was no sign of this at the time. However, what is also clear,
looking back, is that his character seemed to fragment.
By then, he was dividing his time between stand-up and
deeply serious films in which he played not just creeps
but killers too. He wasn't making comedies anymore. Nor,
when interviewed, was he his usual lively self. If he wasn't

putting on the fast-talking manic act, he was speaking so slowly he was coming across as catatonically depressed. Robin the clown still appeared occasionally but alongside him was a more serious character, barely able to raise a smile, let alone mock all of the ills of the world. It was a far cry from the days of *Mork & Mindy*.

More inferior films followed, including the sci-fi number *The Final Cut* (2004), a sub-Matrix number in which he played an 'editor' who edited people's memories. Williams deliberated on his joint role as serious actor/comedian. 'It [comedy] gives you a kind of fearlessness, because you know that to go out and do it you have to be ready to put your arse on the line,' he told the *Sydney Morning Herald* in 2004. 'Directors say they like working with comics, usually because they're not afraid to try stuff. They have to [be prepared to] do anything to get the laugh. They are shameless on that level, but also fearless.' Why no more on-screen comedies though? 'It's hard to find a script where you can kick out that hard, and if you do people say: "That's not the role, you know."'

Accessing all this darkness from within cannot have been easy. He was changing physically too. Of course, everyone starts to look different as they grow older but Robin appeared to be shrinking. By the time of his death, a decade on, he was about half the size he'd been in his twenties. Never what you might call a snappy dresser, he started to lose interest in his appearance, was often bearded and, while not unkempt as such, certainly seemed to have made no effort to brush up. Hindsight is a wonderful thing but, looking back over his life, this is when everything began to change.

And the reason was grief. He had been hard hit by the death of his mother three years previously: 'Marsha and I are both orphans now,' he said. 'When my parents died, I never thought they would. My mother was so full of life. The next thing you know, she is a husk. My father too – he almost died and was, like, brought back to life and he said, "Why did you do that?"' Like so many others of his generation, he was seeing his parents live to extreme old age, with very painful results. And then he lost them; the grief ran deep.

And now came another loss that delivered a body blow. His close friend Christopher Reeve had been working as a director on an animated film, *Everyone's Hero* (2006), when, in October 2004, he died suddenly and unexpectedly of cardiac arrest. (Almost unimaginably, given they had a young son, his non-smoking wife Dana was to die of lung cancer, just two years later.)

Robin was poleaxed with grief. The death of any friend at any age is a hard cross to bear but this was a particularly tragic end. Reeve was only fifty-two when he died but his physical decline had been a sad one to behold. One of the most handsome actors of his generation, his nine years in a wheelchair had left him a shadow of his former self, almost unrecognisable from the striking Superman. There was no rhyme or reason to be had from any of it: Christopher was a universally liked figure, generous to a fault and well thought of. To succumb to such a fate seemed beyond cruelty.

'It's hard for me to believe he's gone because he was such a fighter and such a strong personality and soul to begin with,' Robin said in a 2004 interview with *CBS*. 'People used to come up to me in New York, I remember, the first time after the accident: "Tell your friend he's amazing!" Guys in the back of a garbage truck: "Tell Chris hello!" Guys yesterday when I was coming in for the ceremony, there were guys standing outside. "My feelings are with you; I'm very sorry about your loss." Just guys, regular people who were sending out their condolences.'

Life went on, as it has to do, but those words couldn't even begin to convey the pain he was feeling. As Dana once said, they were more like brothers than friends. They had started out together when they were young and the world lay before them, forming the bond that only comes after decades of shared memories. And this is how it was to end. Life felt exceedingly bleak and all the comedy, all the gaming, all the cycling and the other distractions couldn't shut out the sadness now engulfing him.

It didn't help that he was making some pretty terrible and almost immediately forgettable films. *The Big White* (2005) involved a travel agent with a wife with Tourette's syndrome, who steals a corpse and pretends it's his long-lost brother. Not exactly *Citizen Kane*. But behind the scenes, and despite whatever misery he might have been feeling, were acts of sheer kindness, not just to the likes of the much-lamented Reeve. In 2004 it was revealed that he had taken the trouble to telephone a dying English Literature teacher called Tim Pechey, whom he had never met but who was a very big fan of Robin's and especially *Dead Poets Society*. They first spoke for thirty minutes on the phone; Robin rang again and also sent him video clips.

Williams clearly made a habit of this. In 2014, shortly after his death, it emerged that, just a few weeks previously, he had made a video for a terminally ill twenty-one-year-old girl called Vivian Waller from Auckland, New Zealand. The video showed Robin blowing her a kiss and saying, 'Hey, girl, what's going down in New Zealand?' He even sang to her. It was way beyond what could be expected of anyone and this just before he finally became overwhelmed by his own problems.

He kept up his charity work for the armed forces too. In December 2004, just two months after Christopher's death, Robin was back in Afghanistan: an experience he related to the *San Francisco Chronicle*. 'Some of the shows in Iraq were indoors,' he explained. 'A lot were outdoors. It's weird when you're doing the shows, like in Iraq we do these shows and everyone's in full camo (camouflage) and we're not – so it's kinda like, "Woooow!" It's weird to see all these different camouflages because in the coalition troops, the coalition of the willing, there's all types of camo. The Australians come with somewhat desert camo, we have desert camo and some guys come straight deployment and they have full green, which I'm going: "Doesn't work here. Nice desert." And then the Air Force has this new blue camouflage. Unless you're up against the sky, what is this s—? Blue, like big time. Even gay people are going, "Like: no. Quail egg, what is it? It's teal, it's teal and white, it's so fabulous!" The shows, we would perform to 2,000 to 3,000 in some places... by the end, it got to be a good rhythm.'

And he was well aware that he was following on a tradition started by Bob Hope during the Second World War. 'Oh, yeah, like a traditional Bob Hope show, kind of, except blue,' he said. 'You know, Bob Hope with a strap-on. The general [chairman of the Joint Chiefs of Staff Gen. Richard B. Myers] opened the show. He was like the hardcore. He sets the tone just to say, hey, thank you. He's very personal because he gets out and meets everyone. In the first year, we went with him. The first year we went alone. It was just USO shows, just me. We did the shows and most times we'd stay in the bases overnight. Like in Afghanistan, we'd stayed. Bagram, Kandahar, Jacobabad [Pakistan] and then a base in Afghanistan. You'd go visit all the bases. When you go with the general, it's in and out. The first time it was just me. Last year it was with the general again, which was fun. You travel on his nickel and you get in and get out. No waiting.'

When he was fifty-three, Robin was awarded a Golden Globe Lifetime Achievement Award, quite possibly a little early, and gave voice to Fender in an animated film called *Robots* (2005). Boasting a cast that included Ewan

McGregor, Halle Berry, Greg Kinnear and Mel Brooks, it was a step up, garnering good reviews and commercial success. This was his first animated film since *Aladdin* and it was a positive experience. As with the earlier film, he ad-libbed, this time around producing over thirty hours of tape, although much of it couldn't be used on the grounds that the material was too blue. 'I guess I got too adult,' he confessed. 'I can't help it. I feel inspired and words just roll off my tongue.'

In the background, however, another huge problem was beginning to re-emerge: during the making of *The Big White* he had fallen off the wagon. For some years now, he'd been drinking again and now it was really starting to take its toll. 'I was in a small town where it's not the edge of the world, but you can see it from there, and then I thought: drinking,' he told the *Guardian*. 'I just thought, hey, maybe drinking will help. Because I felt alone and afraid. It was that thing of working so much, and going fuck, maybe that will help. And it was the worst thing in the world.

'You feel warm and kind of wonderful. And then the next thing you know, it's a problem, and you're isolated.'

There it was again, that vulnerability coming out: he felt alone and afraid. What did Williams have to be afraid of? Still a massive star, he could sell out mega-venues and was a big enough name to get a film going on the strength of his involvement alone. Plus he had a secure family unit in the background. But the little boy was still there and it seemed his problems were not going to go away.

In actual fact, what really started the initial relapse were concerns about his career. He could scarcely ignore the fact that his films were getting terrible reviews, with a lot of them not doing well at the box office either. Hollywood could forgive any amount of sentimentality but it would not accept failure and that was what he was really beginning to fear. It had happened to countless others, after all. Yet another of the stresses about being an A-lister is that, when you reach the top, there's an awfully long way to fall down. Nor is there any lack of detractors happy to kick you as you do so.

'*The Big White*,' Williams recalled of the film that had him raiding the mini-bars again. 'It was shot in Skagway [Alaska], this tiny town. It's not the end of the world, but you can see it from there. The movie was interesting, but I was worried. My film career was not going too well. One day I walked into a store and saw a little bottle of Jack Daniel's. And then that voice – I call it the "lower power" – goes, "Hey. Just a taste. Just one." I drank it, and there was that brief moment of "Oh, I'm okay!" But it escalated so quickly. Within a week, I was buying so many bottles I sounded like a wind chime walking down the street. I knew it was really bad one Thanksgiving when I was so drunk they had to take me upstairs.'

He denied that Christopher Reeve's death made it a lot worse but then we cannot always tell why we act as we do. 'No,' he told the *Guardian* when that was put to him, 'it's more selfish than that. It's just literally being afraid. And you think, oh, this will ease the fear. And it doesn't.' What caused the fear? 'Everything. It's just a general all-round arggghhh. It's fearfulness and anxiety.'

According to him, he realised almost immediately that this wasn't going to be pretty, although he carried on for another three years. 'For that first week you lie to yourself, and tell yourself you can stop, and then your body kicks back and says no, stop later. And then it took about three years, and finally you do stop. Most of the time you just realise you've started to do embarrassing things.' He recalled drinking at a charity auction hosted by Sharon Stone at Cannes: 'And I realised I was pretty baked, and I look out and I see all of a sudden a wall of paparazzi. And I go, "Oh well, I guess it's out now".'

At least he stayed off the coke. 'I knew that would kill me,' he continued. 'No. Cocaine – paranoid and impotent, what fun! There was no bit of me thinking, ooh, let's go back to that. Useless conversations until midnight, waking up at dawn feeling like a vampire on a day pass. No.'

But the drink was doing for him. Williams favoured vodka – many an alcoholic's choice – and started having blackouts, unable to remember what he had said or done the next day.

By 2006 his life was in upheaval and his marriage in serious trouble. 'You know, I was shameful, and you do stuff that causes disgust, and that's hard to recover from,' he admitted later. 'You can say, "I forgive you" and all that stuff, but it's not the same as recovering from it. It's not coming back.' Under pressure from his family, he checked into rehab, specifically Oregon's Hazelden Springbrook treatment centre, where he stayed for two months, drying out. He had also been unnerved by what had happened to Mel Gibson, another actor who spent decades fighting alcohol problems and who had just been arrested for driving under the influence – naturally, he was concerned a similar thing could happen to him. Locals who saw him during his stay reported that he appeared very subdued and haggard. He was clearly in a bad way.

In fact, he was worse than he himself had realised. 'Williams originally entered a 30-day treatment programme,' a source told the *Sun*. 'But after the initial 30 days were up, he realised that he needed another 30 days of inpatient treatment to get his life under control. During the last 30 days, he lived in a house near the rehab centre specifically set up for after-care patients. He was still required to attend daily AA meetings and appointments with his counsellors.' After he left, he did not return to the family home but rather rented an apartment in Los Angeles. 'Instead of going home to his wife and two teenage children in Napa Valley, he's moved to Los Angeles, where he's renting an apartment and living with a "sober companion",' said the source. 'Williams hired the companion to watch over him 24 hours a day and ensure he doesn't fall off the wagon.' At that stage he was still hoping he could rescue his relationship with Marsha but it was not to be.

'It waits,' he told *Good Morning America* in 2006. 'It lays in wait for the time when you think, "It's fine now, I'm OK." Then, the next thing you know, it's not OK. Then you realize, "Where am I? I didn't realize I was in Cleveland."' The stint in rehab was enough to get him sober again (although not, this time, for two decades – there was to be a final slip) but the damage was already done and his marriage was beyond repair. Finally, the partnership that had worked so well on a personal and professional level was about to end.

Somehow, in the midst of all this, Williams continued to work. He was still worrying about his career and now he was being offered nothing like the choice roles he'd had in the past but his output continued to be steady. Next up was *House of D* (2004), directed by David Duchovny (and also featuring his daughter Zelda). It told the story of thirteen-year-old Tommy and his friend Pappass (Williams), a middle-aged man with the same mental age. The attempt to stop playing damaged children trapped in the body of an older man was not going so well. Somewhat ominously billed as a 'coming-of-age comedy drama' – the film was, alas, another turkey. At this stage in the game, he could have done with an even break.

Nevertheless, consummate professional that he was, Williams dutifully gave interviews to publicise the project. 'I just did the research about a high-functioning mentally handicapped,' he told *Cinema Confidential* in 2005. 'Socially adept, but intellectually and emotionally not that adept in certain situations, intellectually about a ten- or eleven-year-old, and physically it was like that capable of doing manual labor and stuff… This is a very specific film, so you want to try and find a range that you haven't seen in most people. People who know, who go, "I know what that is." And other people who kind of look around and go, "Oh, that's different." I mean, he's very verbal, but he's slow with certain things. He's able to understand and pick up what's going on emotionally, but it's an arrested development at a certain stage, maybe about ten or eleven.' And, as he didn't say, 'again'.

But it had been fun working with Zelda, who played Melissa, with whom Tommy becomes interested. Her father was certainly proud. 'She was so good in the movie *House of D*,' he said happily. 'She was so instinctual. I was playing a character that was mentally challenged. I am kind of sitting there watching her and at the same time saying, she is good. She has the same kind of mental quickness but she is also sensitive. The greatest compliment of all was that she was not only a good actress; she was also kind to people. She treated all the other kids well. She ate lunch with everybody. She did not have an attitude with them and was decent with all the crew. People said, "Your daughter is good but she is also nice." That is kind of the double bill.'

And then there came *The Night Listener* (2006). From the original book by Armistead Maupin (of *Tales of the City* fame), it's the story of a DJ who befriends a little boy on the telephone but comes to doubt that he really exists. It was another very mixed bag. Listening to interviews from the time, Williams was beginning to sound far more subdued, even when he can't help himself and starts putting on silly voices again. But he was now hinting at far deeper problems too. 'Do I perform sometimes in a manic style? Yes,' he told Terry Goss in a radio interview. 'Am I manic all the time? No. Do I get sad? Oh, yeah. Does it hit me hard? Oh, yeah… No clinical depression, no. No. I get bummed, like I think a lot of us do at certain times. You look at the world and go, "Whoa!" Other moments you look and go, "Oh, things are OK."'

The deaths of his parents, his friend Christopher Reeve's death, drinking, rehab and now a failing marriage… He was now caught up in a maelstrom that, at times, seemed to be hurtling out of control. Then there was the undeniable fact that his career was not what it was: he had made some pretty awful movies and no one seemed to want to let him forget that. 'Why?' The *Guardian* asked. Just why had he chosen to do so?

Williams rallied – briefly. 'Well, I've had a lot of people tell me they watched *Old Dogs* with their kids and had a good time.' Then he fessed up. 'No, it paid the bills. Sometimes you have to make a movie to make money. You know what you're getting into, totally. You know they're going to make it goofy. And that's OK.' But was it really OK? After all, he was a Juilliard-trained actor, someone who took his craft seriously. And there were quite a few audiences who didn't think that it was all right at all. When you have tasted the glory, it is hard to cope with the second rate.

Alas, more dross followed – *Man of the Year* with Christopher

Walken (2006), *RV* (also 2006), which barely lasted in the cinema a couple of months before going straight to DVD – all the trauma of recent years may well have affected his judgment in that he took part in so much that was so bad. Perhaps it was due to the fact that another costly divorce was clearly on the horizon but, in 2004 and 2005, he appeared in three films each, while in 2006 he was in an astonishing six movies. That's a huge amount of work and either he badly needed the money or he was using the work to ignore what else was wrong in his life. At any rate, something was going on but, in among all the forgettable films, some gems showed signs of surviving the test of time. Though not his own vehicles, they certainly benefited from his input.

The first of these was *Night At The Museum* (2006), which was actually a Ben Stiller vehicle (if Williams resented playing second fiddle to a younger comic actor who was playing a role that he himself might have been given a few years previously, he had the good sense not to say so). Stiller played Larry Daley, a security guard at the American Museum of Natural History, who discovers that the exhibits come to life at night. Theodore Roosevelt (Robin) explains the reason for this to him and, over time, Larry learns how to control the mayhem. The film received mixed reviews but it was a huge commercial success – and was credited with increasing visitor numbers to the real American Museum of Natural History. Robin was not that keen on sequels but he was to appear in another two to this film, including one that has yet to be released.

The second project, *Happy Feet* (2006), also spawned a sequel. This was an animated film about penguins, in which Robin voiced Ramón and Lovelace. Ostensibly, it was mainly a jolly lark but one with a strong environmental message: 'You can't tell a story about Antarctica and the penguins without giving that dimension,' said director George Miller. Not only did the film garner good reviews, it actually beat *Casino Royale*, starring Daniel Craig as the latest incarnation of James Bond, to the top slot at the box office. It also won a slew of awards, including an Oscar for Best Animated Film.

Robin reprised his role in the sequel (unimaginatively titled *Happy Feet Two*, 2011) and, whatever his feelings about sequels or no, this particular series sparked quite a serious discussion about the environment – one that continues to this day. It is ironic that a man so often accused of overt sentimentality ended up in a film that was, on the face of it, a children's movie, but a far more serious treatise lay underneath.

More films followed, not always worthy of mention, but, whatever his workload, he couldn't shy away from the inevitable any longer. That three-year drinking binge had taken its toll and the estrangement from Marsha was complete. Robin, the needy child who couldn't bear to be alone, was heading for his second divorce.

> *Gus: Keep a lid on it butterscotch.*
>
> NIGHT AT THE MUSEUM (2006)

CHAPTER THIRTEEN

A FRESH
START?

*'Ah, yes, divorce… from the Latin word meaning to rip
out a man's genitals through his wallet.'*
ROBIN WILLIAMS

Williams might have been hoping to save his marriage but there had been too much stress to deal with and, in March 2008, Marsha filed for divorce, citing irreconcilable differences. In total, he was to end up with a £20 million bill – no joke, even for someone who was seriously rich. 'I get on fabulously with my exes – now we're not together any more. And they always appreciated my body hair, which was a plus, obviously,' he told the *Daily Telegraph*, evidently attempting to make light of things.

In reality, however, there was a lot more going on. Robin

compared being married to a comedian with owning a cobra. 'Basically, there's a certain amount of novelty, and the novelty is showing the cobra to your friends – but comics can be nasty,' he admitted. 'Along with our desperate insecurity, sometimes we're equipped to be vicious.'

But joking aside, this was really no laughing matter. Marsha had been a real source of stability for Robin: four years after they got together he gave an interview to the *New York Times* in 2008 in which he said, 'I don't need to go out to a club now and get a little bit of intimacy from 100 or 200 people. Now I can get that talking to friends around the table.' She had done that. His former wife had also helped shape his career and, while it hadn't been doing so well in recent years, she had been heavily involved in projects including *Mrs. Doubtfire* and *Robin Williams Live On Broadway*. They had been involved in the Windfall Foundation together, hosted numerous fundraisers and encouraged each other in their own charitable enterprises, Marsha's particular causes being Doctors Without Borders and Seacology. She was also the mother of two of his children and had previously helped him when he had been in a very bad place.

Robin was to marry for a third time and it would be quite wrong to imply that Susan Schneider, his third wife, meant any less to him than Marsha. But the separation from Marsha marked a seismic shift in his life. They had been together not only through his reign at the top of the Hollywood A-list but also the pain of his first divorce and had shared the happiness of family life. For two decades Marsha had been at the centre of Robin's world and the break-up was a terrible blow. At the root of it, he was so very unhappy and insecure and it came about at a point when his career was in the doldrums. This was not a good time.

Although neither had said anything publicly, in fact, there had been signs for some time that all was not well. In 2007 Williams was honoured by the San Francisco International Film Festival with the Peter J. Owens Award but, strangely, Marsha wasn't by his side. She issued a very gracious statement after Robin's death but there was clearly a great deal of hurt on both sides. Now in his mid-fifties, he was having to deal with the issue of ageing (not easy for anyone). He insisted it didn't matter, telling *Philippine News Online*, 'I don't really think about old age. I acknowledge that at a certain age, there are things that all of a sudden you start to realize I did not hear that. Or, you have a senior moment where you go, what is my name? Oh Robin. Yeah right.' Life was proving remarkably tough.

To make matters worse, Robin's oldest half-brother, Robert Todd Williams – 'Toad' – died in 2007 after complications on the back of heart surgery (something he himself would later undergo). There was yet more cause for great sadness – while the three half-brothers had not been close as children, they had become so as adults and Robin was very distressed. Somewhat ironically, given Robin's recent struggles with alcohol, Toad ran Toad Hollow, a famously winery, called one of his saloons Risky

Liver Inn (in private, at least!) and, as Robin said of him, 'Toad left a big footprint with a cork, or as a friend said, he left a great trail.' A larger-than-life bon viveur, he would be greatly missed.

By this time, Christopher Reeve's widow Dana had also passed away: another tragedy that totally floored Williams, not least because she left behind a young son. And so he did what he so often did when life seemed to be getting the better of him: he went back to stand-up. In 2008 he announced that he was to embark on a twenty-six-city stand-up tour entitled *Weapons Of Self Destruction*, a very obvious reference to his recent woes. Many, many more dates were to be added and the tour went to the UK and Australia. There was some speculation that he was doing it because he needed the money but, whatever the truth, several elements stood out. The first was that stand-up had always offered some sort of refuge in troubled times and those were troubled times indeed.

His old friend Billy Crystal certainly thought so. 'Over the last couple of years and the pain that he's gone through, his brain is the one thing that's kept him buoyant,' he told *The Guardian* in 2009 'I think he needs the stand-up in a different way than he did before. It's still a safe place for him to be, but he can talk about things and make himself feel better, not just everybody else.'

The second was that, whatever travails he might be experiencing in his film career, his stand-up act was as popular as it had ever been. Almost instantly, the tour sold out – not bad going for a man in his late fifties. Williams the film actor might be having problems but Williams the stand-up was as adored as he had ever been. Indeed, this was always the case: public affection for Robin never wavered, right up until the end of his life.

It was something he experienced when he went out on the road. 'I just walked around and most people were like: "Oh, hi, how are you?"' he told the *Robin Williams Fansite*. 'Ninety-nine per cent of the people are so sweet.

'The only time I run into people who violate that boundary are drunks. And having been one, I get it, but I don't need to tolerate it. Like, I was walking... he wasn't even drunk. There was a guy who all of a sudden started grabbing me to make a picture with his cell phone and I said: "Let go." He kept grabbing me and I went: "No, no, I know your English isn't great, but don't grab me." I'll take a picture with you. Treat me like a person and not like a prop. And most people do that.'

It was an illustration of the fact that he could never be anonymous; of course, something he had lived with for years. But it also meant that, when he experienced difficulties, it had to be very public.

The tour kicked off in September 2008, with Robin now openly saying that he was doing it for the money – he didn't like the film roles he was being offered. Among the usual targets, he also talked quite openly about his recent travails ('Poor me, poor me… pour me a drink!') But even this was not quite so straightforward as it seemed.

The comic Eric Idle, who had known him for a long time, put his finger on it: 'I've always felt that Robin's blinding speed and flash of wit was an effort at concealment, rather than revealing,' he said. 'He would be talking about something personal or sexual, but it was always in general, not about him.'

He had certainly lost none of his renowned antipathy to George W. Bush – 'The Bush library will be interactive – which is code for, Not So Many Books' – and was happy to talk about the new President as well: 'Obama is an amazing combination of Martin Luther King and Spock.' And he was just as funny as ever; he still had the capacity to reduce audiences to tears of laughter. On stage, as he himself so often observed, he didn't need to deal with real life.

But if he was, at least in part, doing this tour to take his mind off his current troubles, life was about to put another on his plate. As the tour went on, he began to experience bouts of breathlessness – no joke when an act is as frenetic as his. He was quieter these days off stage but on stage quite the firebrand he had always been and, by February and March of the following year, had developed a cough as well. As it became increasingly obvious that something was wrong, he consulted his physician. At first, he appeared to have a respiratory complaint and then it became clear that the problem was actually with his heart. An angiogram followed, which revealed that he needed a heart bypass and, in March 2009, after postponing some tour dates, he went in for surgery at the Cleveland Clinic in Ohio, before going home for a few weeks to recover. He had one aorta replaced with a cow's valve, which, of course, was to be the basis of a great many more jokes.

'I would finish shows and all of sudden I would be going, "Wow, I am really kind of rundown",' he told the *New Zealand Herald*. 'It wasn't like normal, where I was tired but feeling great. So I was in Miami, about to do some shows, and it was "No, no, you have to get this looked at. You have two weeks to decide where you want to have your surgery". That was like, "Beep! Put the brakes on and do the valve grind", which I think sounds like a great sexual dance. The tour really kind of pointed out, "You have got to do something about this, pal".'

For Robin it was second nature to joke. In reality, however, it just served to heighten his sense of melancholia. He had 'a bit of fear' that the surgery would kill him, he told *The New York Times* in 2009, adding, 'I think, literally, because you have cracked the chest, you are vulnerable, totally, for the first time since birth. It's like, oh, don't get weepy now. My children! My babies.'

In the event, the operation was a total success but it could not have come at a worse moment. He had already been having a torrid time of it, something he was dealing with by being on stage, and to have to stay at home with only his thoughts for company was not a recipe for happiness. He needed to work and he needed to be out there and there was a sense of great relief when he was once more permitted to tour.

Williams was keen, however, to show that he was back on form. Eight weeks after the operation, he released a picture of himself with his T-shirt pulled up, displaying a huge scar that ran the whole way down his chest. He then appeared on David Letterman's show to explain what had happened to him, throwing in a few riffs along the way. 'I realise now that shortness of breath is kind of code for heart problem,' he admitted, 'just like exhaustion is code for alcoholic. Yeah, I'm going to Betty Ford for exhaustion. I'm taking a nap!

'I'm ethanol challenged. I would walk up a flight of stairs and all of a sudden I realised, "I'm old". But something was off and I went in and they did a stress test and I walked on the treadmill. I have one new valve and a repaired valve. I have a cow valve and the grazing's been fun. And I give a good quarter cream too. It's from the heart of a cow. They give you a choice – you can have a pig valve and then find truffles, or a cow valve. The mechanical valves last much longer. It's great but, if someone uses a remote control, you fart.' Oh and, 'It really makes you appreciate the little things, like breathing.' That was Robin and, with that, he was back on the road again.

'I took three months off, and after the three months I was like, "I think I can do this",' he told *Star Adviser*. 'One night I went on stage a little early, about a month or two into the recovery time, and I was out of breath and I went, "Not ready, not ready. Warning." Then after the three months, I went, "No, I can do it." It's slightly slower than I was before but not by much. Only a few people would notice, but you do take it a little bit slower.'

He was to spend quite a bit of time touring, with the act inevitably ending up as an HBO special and, although he'd complained about the quality of the work being offered, the films continued to pour out too. And it is not true to say that they were all bad. 'I have been doing small movies,' he told the *New Zealand Herald*. 'Small movies are great to do, but they don't pay the bills. Literally. You do them and they are great to do, and I am very proud of them but it doesn't pay the overheads. Even the guy I did the last movie with, Bobcat Goldthwait, the director, he's a comic too. He has to go out and play clubs. I'm playing auditoriums. We are both making money the old-fashioned way.'

And what, he was asked, of the duds? 'You don't rue them. There are some you go, "Maybe you shouldn't have made that", but you did. There are some that are wonderful, some that are not so good and some that you go "Woah!" And usually the ones that didn't work were the ones where someone said, "This is going to be a hit." That is the most frightening one – where you went into it for the wrong motivation – to make shitloads of cash.'

There it was – that reference to money again. Despite all the initial speculation after Williams' death, it really does not seem that he was in financial difficulties, expensive though the divorces had been, not least because he still had a few films to come out. What is far more likely is that he was becoming obsessed with the fear of running out of cash – something quite different – which is why he talked about it so much. But when you enter a period of darkness, everything seems hopeless, although he wasn't quite there yet.

That film he referred to making with Goldthwait was, in fact, a massive return to form. The two of them made *World's Greatest Dad*, which was quite on a par with some of his finest films in the past and garnered the best reviews he'd had in years. As a small, art-house movie, it only received limited theatrical release but it showed him at his sharpest, a world away from his more sentimental material. It was a comedy but it was very, very dark. Robin played Lance, an English literature teacher who was pretty much the opposite of his character in *Dead Poets Society*, given that he taught a poetry class everyone hated. A failed novelist, desperate to be published, he was a single parent to his obnoxious son Kyle (Daryl Sabara) and engaged in a desultory relationship with a fellow teacher, who was also dating a considerably more successful teacher at the school.

One night, Lance returns home to discover that Kyle has accidentally killed himself in an act of auto-erotic asphyxiation and, in order to save his son embarrassment, he makes it appear as if he has hung himself the more traditional way, as well as forging a suicide note. This note achieves a cult status at the school, as does Kyle's journal, which Lance has forged. Lance himself experiences a huge shift: his pupils start to respect him and he also appears on television as the media become increasingly interested in the story. The only person who is suspicious is Kyle's friend Andrew (Evan Martin), who thinks the moving note and journal extremely uncharacteristic of his friend. When the principal announces that the school library is to be renamed after Kyle, Lance can take it no more and confesses what he has done. Though renounced by everyone, he is free.

Patch Adams it was not but it marked a massive return to form. If Williams had stuck to films like this, he would have had to endure a great deal less criticism than some of his choices garnered – although, as he himself admitted, the film was never going to be a big money spinner – because people loved it. *World's Greatest Dad* was shown at the Sundance Film Festival in Utah. 'Lusciously perverse, and refreshingly original comedy that tackles love, loss, and our curious quest for infamy,' was the verdict, while Robin was praised for his outstanding performance. It was 'brilliant', 'genius' and 'one of the best films of the year', said the critics.

'A startlingly excellent dark comedy about the power of positive posthumous PR. One of 2010's must-see movies,' wrote Catherine Bray. 'Goldthwait's pacing is uncertain, and his humour is frequently "off", but the sense of risky provocation is compelling,' opined Anthony Quinn in *The Independent*. And the message was clear: Williams still had what it takes. If only he would choose his other projects a little more carefully. However – and it was a *big* however – the film was not a massive hit, almost certainly because of the subject matter.

Goldthwait initially enlisted Robin as a friend, not the potential lead, to see if he could help him to get the film into production. 'I read it to say, "Look, let me see if I can help get this made for you." Because when he did Shakes the Clown, I played Jerry the Mime as a favour, and it was like, let me see what I can play... and then I thought, "No, this is really good."'

He was aware, though, that they were dealing with a difficult subject matter. 'Dealing with the loss of a child, I can't imagine... so that's kind of difficult to think of. But the script was fearless and we had to go that way. You can't be glib about it. You can't be like, "Hey, my kid was a prick. He's dead. So what?" You can't go that way.' And then there was the tidying up scene... 'Yeah and clean up after his kid. And try and y'know... even the idea of zipping up his fly and putting away every bit of evidence, it's like, "Okay, how we gonna deal with this, coach?"'

Things seemed to be looking up. Robin had a new wife, Susan Schneider, whom he'd met in an Apple Store. 'I was wearing camouflage pants, and she said, "How's that camouflage working?" I said, "Pretty good, because you noticed." I had this weird feeling, so I said, "I know this sounds like a horrible pickup line, but I feel like I know you." And she said, "Yeah, me too." And then we realized we had a common theme in sobriety,' he told *People Magazine*. They'd met in 2009, just before Robin discovered he would need surgery and Susan, a San Francisco-based graphic designer, proved a keeper, looking after him as he recovered. Fifteen years younger than him and five inches taller, she was also a painter and brought some much-needed happiness back into his life.

The relationship turned serious pretty quickly: they married in 2011 at the Meadowood Resort in St Helena, California, and honeymooned in Paris. Williams was a man who needed female companionship: he'd never had the slightest problem attracting women but he required something more stable than a few casual flings that didn't mean anything.

'No, Apple. A-p-p-l-e store; we were both looking for weird technology and our eyes met and we just got married last month, which, given my track record, is a bit like bringing a burns victim to a fireworks display,' he said on another occasion to the *Daily Telegraph*. The couple now lived in Robin's mother's old home: 'I've done the ranch thing, now I'm doing the water thing where I go kayaking and paddleboarding and take to the woods for hours on my bike. It's my thinking time and very therapeutic. I also have a gay rescue pug called Leonard, who I take for walks, because I am very secure in my sexuality. He has a boyfriend and they are planning to adopt a Siamese kitten together. We're very modern.'

It was a new family; you didn't need to be a psychologist to guess that Robin was almost certainly trying to replace the one he had lost.

He continued to worry about money, however. 'I've never been asked to appear on *I'm a Celebrity… Get Me Out of*

Here!' he mused, 'so I guess I mustn't be on the professional skids just yet,' he told the *Daily Telegraph*. 'Besides, I would never appear on it. Never. I don't do well with snakes and I can't dance. I am such a bad dancer, in fact, that I could only ever appear on a telethon, raising money for damaged people: "The phone lines are open. Pledge us money and We Will Make Him Stop".' He seemed to have mistakenly confused *I'm a Celebrity…* with *Strictly Come Dancing* but the fretting was there nonetheless.

The renewed stability in his private life, allied to the fact that he was making some decent films, seemed to have opened Williams to the possibility of taking a risk. It was now years since that less-than-successful outing with *Waiting For Godot* at the Lincoln Center but, in 2011, he trod the boards once more in Rajiv Joseph's *Bengal Tiger at the Baghdad Zoo* at the Richard Rodgers Theatre, his Broadway debut. The wife of his manager, David Steinberg, had introduced him to the play. Heavily bearded (a look he sported a lot in those days), Robin played the tiger, a beast guarded by two American soldiers in the early days of the war in Iraq. The tiger talks to the audience and continues to do so after a soldier has shot and killed it. *Bengal Tiger* was a brave play and it was a brave man who took on the role. Again, he garnered excellent reviews.

'But Mr Williams, the kinetic comic who has sometimes revealed a marshmallowy streak in movies, never indulges the audience's hunger for displays of humorous invention or pinpricks of poignancy,' wrote Charles Isherwood in

The New York Times. 'He gives a performance of focused intelligence and integrity, embodying the animal who becomes the play's questioning conscience with a savage bite that never loosens its grip.' This was, in fact, considerably better than the days of *Godot*: once again, he was receiving the professional acclaim he so craved.

'It just hit me hard, it was so powerful,' Robin told *The New York Times*. 'I read it, and I was going: "I'm in. I can come into it and create it from the ground up." And I'm hairy enough to be a tiger, so that's good. Most of the time, most of the characters are, to be blunt, ghosts. I mean, I don't want to spoil it – 'This is what it's about' – but right off the bat, you're in Iraq, it's all these ghosts wandering around, talking and gaining more consciousness as they continue through the play.'

He had, of course, actually been to Iraq, when he was entertaining US troops. 'The last time I was [in Iraq] I stayed in [Saddam Hussein's son] Uday's hunting lodge, although the only thing he hunted was Russian hookers,' he told *TIME Magazine* in an interview in 2011. 'It was like if Hitler had built Graceland; it was so tacky. Even Colombian drug lords are going, "This is some tacky stuff." But my feelings about the war are about ghosts. I was just there recently, and [everything is] "winding down." What do you leave there when it just ends? There's a line in the play: "The Americans think when something dies, that's it, it's over." But when you go to the Middle East, you realize there's a real sense that things stay around.'

219

It was, in fact, a triumph and he received a great deal of acclaim. Again and again, he was showing he'd still got it, in every field he touched. But that nagging insecurity about money continued and, along with choosing to sell his beautiful ranch in Marin County, Robin decided he wanted a regular income.

He was going back to where it all began – a regular series on TV.

> 'On stage you're free. You can say and do things that if you said and did any place else, you'd be arrested.'
> ROBIN WILLIAMS

CHAPTER FOURTEEN

SHADOWS
FALL

*'You know you get that tattoo of barbed wire when you're
eighteen? By the time you're eighty, it's a picket fence.'*
ROBIN WILLIAMS

Williams continued to adjust to his new life. His children
had grown up and left home now – although in the wake
of the divorce their base had been with Marsha anyway -
so it was just Robin, Susan and the dogs. In the old days,
he had enjoyed the scrum of the family but, even if he
and Marsha hadn't divorced, life was changing. He was
growing older and life moved at a different pace.

'It's quiet,' he told *MSN Today* in 2011. 'I just saw
my daughter, Zelda, the other night. My oldest son is
married, and my youngest son just went off to college.
It's like they've left the earth's gravity, and I'm watching

them. "There he gooooes!" I'm just so proud. I don't have a college degree, and my father didn't have a college degree, so when my son, Zachary, graduated from college, I said, "My boy's got learnin'!"'

Of course, the immensely erudite Robin had learning too – lots of it.

And he was proud of his children. 'I have to give credit to my ex, Marsha,' he told *Parade*. 'She did the majority of the work on that level. She really tries to ground them and protect them, but not overly so. There were three years [drinking] when I was pretty out. Now I really have to be there for them. The most important thing to say is "If you need me, I'm here." Zelda's acting in small movies and writing, which is wonderful. Cody is doing music production. Zachary's married and working. When he graduated from NYU, it was one of the most moving days of my life. I was so proud of him. Because I don't have a college degree.'

It was odd that Robin was obsessing so much about this now: in midlife, perhaps he had got to a stage of brooding about what might have been.

Meanwhile, the films continued to pour out. He reprised his dual role in *Happy Feet Two* (2011): 'Well, you have to do it better than the first time to make it worthwhile, not just for the sake of the franchise,' he told *MSN Today*. '[Director] George [Miller] kicked it hard. I asked him after he saw it what he thought, and he said, "Well, I don't know, but I think it's better." I said, "I think so, too." He used the technology, performances, everything, and took it to a new level.'

There was the usual ad-libbing: 'There was one moment as Lovelace where I started speaking in tongues. I got so kind of crazy that I almost passed out. George said, "That's great. Keep going!" I told him that if I kept going, I would fall down. I just started doing this Baptist hymnal thing. "Hmmmmhmmmmhmmmm." I think that's actually what led to the gospel song that's in the movie.'

Then there was another film (though, alas, not one of his better choices): *The Angriest Man in Brooklyn* (2014). The story involves an obnoxious man who has a car accident and is so unpleasant to the doctor in the hospital he is sent to that she tells him he has only ninety minutes to live. Queue the patient charging around the place, trying to right the wrongs he has committed in record time, while the doctor, realising that she could be struck off, charges round, trying to find him.

The reviews were pitiless. 'A schmaltz opera that indulges Robin Williams' most melancholy tics and themes,' wrote Peter Debruge in *Variety*. 'The film never quite manages to figure out what it's actually about,' declared Bilge Ebiri in *New York Magazine/Vulture*. 'The movie is predictably sentimental at its root, but it's also meant to be comedy, partly resting on Mr Williams's energetic but failed attempt to play a jerk,' said Nicolas Rapold in *The New York Times*. 'Every scene between two people comes off like drunkenly shot video of a play rehearsal gone horribly wrong,' opined Robert Abele in *The Los Angeles Times*.

'Robin Williams once again proves he can insufferably crank the energy to 11 without batting an eye, only this time his frenzied comic demeanor is replaced with equally harried contempt,' said Drew Hunt of *Slant Magazine*. 'As broad as Williams goes in these scenes, it's not really his fault. He's acting out a screenplay, credited to Daniel Taplitz, that's peppered with bad writerly flourishes,' wrote Jesse Hassenger of *AV Club*.

Ouch! To a somewhat oversensitive man, this was not a pretty read.

That said, along with the brickbats, there were plenty of bouquets flying Williams' way. He was invited to The Paley Center for Media for an evening in his honour, sponsored by *TV Guide*.

'I never think of myself as a legend,' said Robin, somewhat wonderingly. 'It's a weird label, like "mythological," with little people behind you [saying], "We worship you." When I started on TV there were only three networks and now there are hundreds. And even though this is my first time at The Paley Center, I know you can come here and see incredible TV from the past.'

Director Bobcat Goldthwait made a speech. 'During my toast at Robin's wedding, I referred to his new wife as a MILF,' he said. 'And I threw him a bachelor party, where a lovely performer named Lady Monster showed up and lit different parts of her anatomy on fire. It's the least I could do for Robin, who has always offered a shoulder for me to cry on when things were bad. We've had a nice run as best pals.'

Some more very small-scale films went on, including *The Face of Love* (2013), in which a woman, Nikki (Annette Bening), falls in love with someone who looks incredibly like her late husband (Ed Harris). Robin played Roger, a close friend who wanted to be something more.

As so often, the filmmakers were thrilled to have Williams on board: 'He's probably one of my favorite people I've ever worked with,' said producer Bonnie Curtis. 'I met Robin when I was twenty-three or twenty-four years old. We did the movie *Hook* [1991] together, which was about a three-year shooting schedule, so we all got to know each other really well. I called up Robin because I thought, for this part, that he would just get this guy.'

She sent him the script and 'he called me up and he said, "Well, now Ed has the really good part." And I agreed, "Yes, he does." And then Robin said, "But I get this guy. I get Roger, and I can do it. I'd love to try, at least." And that was really it. He was absolutely precious. He told me that he based it on an actual occurrence that happened to his mother, seeing a man who looked exactly like his father and how that affected her, and that he'd built it from that, which is kind of beautiful. The tone is very sweet. At the same time, there's great depth and sadness. This stuff is very passionate, and very palpable.'

There was absolutely nothing wrong with doing this sort

of film – it was art-house territory, with an interesting plot and well worth making – but it was not the mega-bucks blockbuster of yesteryear and Williams had worked himself into a state about money. Life was pretty depressing in other ways, too. The comedian and actor Jonathan Winters had just died and Williams paid a gracious tribute to his friend in the way that, alas, so many of his contemporaries would soon do for him too.

'Jonathan Winters was my mentor. I once told him that and he said, "Please. I prefer 'Idol.'" But I knew it was true. I knew the moment I saw him on *The Tonight Show* when Jack Paar handed him a stick. What happened next was a genius at play. John and that stick transformed into a dozen different characters, complete with sound effects – a fly-fisherman, a matador, Bing Crosby playing a round of golf ... he was comedy at the speed of thought and I was hooked.

'Twenty years later I got to play Jonathan's dad on *Mork & Mindy*. His riffs on our show were like epic mini-movies. Sometimes I would join in and jamming with Jonathan was like dancing with Fred Astaire. He always brought out your best.

'The beauty of Jonathan was that he was a big, brilliant kid that never grew up and the world was his playground. In April, Johnny turned out the lights, but he sure burned bright while he was here. Thanks for the spark, big guy.'

But that was not the only sad news. Robin was still a keen cyclist but now his good friend Lance Armstrong had become caught up in a drugs scandal when it was discovered that he had been taking illicit performance-enhancing drugs.

'I got involved [in cycling] because I couldn't run anymore,' Robin told *Parade* in 2013. 'I loved running, but all of a sudden everything hurt so much. I started cycling when Zelda was born. When I met Lance, I was [already] a cycling fan. I went to five Tours de France and followed his team. That's why it was so disheartening when [the doping scandal] went down.'

Did he feel betrayed? 'It wasn't just Lance. [Most of the] team was doping. I haven't seen him since one of the last Livestrong benefits, I think just before the Oprah interview. It was literally like a wake for someone who was still alive, this overall feeling that the dream was over.'

The world of television was abuzz. David E. Kelley, the man behind such TV classics as *Picket Fences*, *Chicago Hope*, *The Practice*, *Ally McBeal* and *Boston Legal* was launching a new series, *The Crazy Ones*, about a man called Simon Roberts who works in advertising with his daughter Sydney at a Chicago agency called Lewis, Roberts + Roberts. There was particular excitement because the actor who was to play Simon would be none other than Robin Williams. The part had been written especially for him. It was the first time that he had appeared in a television series since *Mork & Mindy*, thirty-one years previously.

The actress playing his daughter Sydney, Sarah Michelle

Gellar, certainly regarded it as a big deal. As soon as she heard Williams would be starring in a new series, she rang a friend of hers called Sarah de Sa Rego, who just happened to be married to Bobcat Goldthwait, to say she wanted to play Sydney. According to Gellar, she 'stalked' Robin: 'I even called his best friend and I was like, "I have to be on this show. Please tell Robin!" I really did!' she said. Her wish was fulfilled. 'He is a legend! Think about it: Greatest stand-up comic of all time, Academy Award winner and nicest man on the planet,' added Gellar.

'It's like if Gandhi did stand-up!' Robin responded.

Like so many before him, he had used television as a platform to launch a film career: so did this feel like a step back? Certainly there was no need for it to feel that way. It was increasingly common for major film stars to appear on television – Alec Baldwin, to name but one, had been a revelation in NBC's *30 Rock*. And David E. Kelley was one of the biggest names in television. There was no conceivable need to fret.

'We needed an actor who could convey genius, insanity, and comedy, tempered with humanity,' Kelley told *Parade* magazine. 'Robin was the first and only choice.'

Robin was certainly enjoying himself. Temporarily relocated with Susan to Los Angeles, he was sounding very enthusiastic. 'It's fun,' he told *Parade*. 'I'm having such a blast doing it with Sarah. She's a sweet woman. And the idea of the father-daughter relationship – since I have a daughter, I've done the research on that. You know, pride and trying to help her along, but at the same time not helping so much that she doesn't learn.'

But there was something else about it that he liked as well. 'The idea of having a steady job is appealing,' said Robin frankly in 2013. 'I have two [other] choices: go on the road doing stand-up, or do small, independent movies working almost for scale [minimum union pay]. The movies are good, but a lot of times they don't even have distribution. There are bills to pay. My life has downsized, in a good way. I'm selling the ranch up in Napa. I just can't afford it anymore.'

The ranch didn't sell – it remained unsold after his death – but there was a truly unhappy note running through all this and, although depression was something Williams had always struggled with, it came out as manic humour, not feeling miserable. 'The idea of you're hot, then you're not,' he said. 'When you're hot, people throw themselves at you. I once got stopped by a cop: "Hi, Mr. Williams. I'm not going to give you a ticket, but I do have an idea for a film."' And when you're not so hot? 'People walk away from you.' He sounded pretty bleak.

Nonetheless, he was prepared to give it his all. His character Simon was, 'a guy who can sell anything. He could sell frappuccinos to Starbucks. He could sell clouds to God. Simon's a guy with a lot of nuance. He's lived hard and been on the edge for a long time. Multiple marriages, rehab, even rehab in wine country. Trust me, I've done the research myself.' The idea was that Simon had been married and divorced a few times, neglecting Sydney as a child, and was now intent on making it up to her as an adult – although she had to prove herself to him before he would take her on. Simon was the manic one, while Sydney was his straight man.

There were more regular characters, not least to provide Sydney with a love interest and to engender a spirit of competition. Pam Dawber, aka Mindy, made a guest appearance towards the end of the season: the first time she and Robin had appeared opposite one another since the old days. So did the new series work? Not really, although all the elements were there.

Everyone involved said they were nervous. *Zap2it* asked Robin how he and Sarah were getting along. 'Very sweetly,' he said. 'I think the first day, we were very honest. I leaned over, and I said, "I'm a little afraid." And she said, "Me, too." I knew there was no audience, which took the pressure off, and then we started doing it.'

And what of James Wolk, who played the womanising copywriter Zach Cropper? 'He's really good,' Robin replied. 'This is a nice thing for him to kick out and be as crazy, as funny as he can, playing this studly character. "Did you sleep with her?" "Not yet." "OK, cool." And they can also pitch with me and throw ideas around and send him in as the designated shtick man, which is kind of wonderful.'

And were the younger actors intimidated by his improvisation? 'Oh, no, they keep up, and they're quicker than me,' insisted Robin. 'They're as quick if not faster. For me, at 62 now ... that's why I've got to find the rhythms, get back up to speed. By the end of the pilot, I was like, "OK, oh, it's over. Now I've got to get back into shape, find the character, find the moments. How outrageous can you be?"'

That was not quite the full story, however, of which more below.

The reviews were, to put it mildly, mixed. 'Williams can't resist falling back on his old bag of tricks on occasion – cartoon voices, gurning, rambling wordplay – but there's a decent amount of pathos to his performance as part-buffoon, part-genius Simon Roberts too and the comedy veteran shares a warm, genuine chemistry with his on-screen offspring Gellar,' said Morgan Jeffery of *Digital Spy*.

Meanwhile, Rob Owen of the *Pittsburgh Post-Gazette* was keeping an open mind: 'Whether *The Crazy Ones* can come together as a series over time remains an open question, but the pilot offers enough charm and humor to warrant future consideration.'

However, Ross Bonaime of *Paste* was cutting: 'I don't know how it does it, but *The Crazy Ones* continues to be one of the most boring comedies with one of the most amazing casts on the air today. The entire show is just treading on "meh." It also feels like this show just exists in a vacuum, with nothing in any prior episode really having an effect on anything that comes after it. There are no continuing story arcs, nor any real characters to really bond with.'

'Created by and executive produced by David E. Kelley, *The Crazy Ones* stars Williams as advertising genius Simon Roberts, while Gellar plays his daughter Sydney, who also happens to be his business partner,' wrote Kelly West in *Cinemablend.com*. 'Roberts is energetic and outlandish in exactly what you'd expect from the frequently riffing funny man, Williams, while Sydney is a bit more reserved, not always eager to follow along with her father's lightning-fast line of thinking and goofy behavior.'

The Boston Herald was probably closest to the mark, saying, 'Williams seems exhausted.'

Given that the constant waterfall of films had by no means dried up, he might well have been exhausted. Now in his sixties, even his superhuman energy surely had its limits. But there was also a sense that he was beginning to give up. He had had a very difficult few years and the depression that was never far away once more held him in thrall.

Worse, according to some people at least, he was drinking again. One scene was shot at a famous watering hole called Wolfgang Puck, in Beverly Hills, home of the power lunch. 'Robin insisted on a real drink,' said a source. 'No one had seen him drinking before this. One drink led to another, but it seemed to calm him down.' If true, this was not good news: not only was he drinking again, he wasn't even attempting to hide it. When he fell off the wagon in 2003, he did at least make some effort to conceal what he was doing, telling bartenders he was buying drinks for someone else. Now, ten years on, he didn't seem to care who knew.

There were other problems as well. Williams had been hired because he was zany and improvisational but, when he started doing the same on set, it was rumoured that the rest of the cast couldn't cope. Sarah Michelle Gellar, in particular, was said to have found it very difficult to work like this, although it must be added that she has never said a word about this publicly and was greatly distressed to hear the news of his death. And it was not like the days of *Mork & Mindy*. Back then, Robin had been an extremely ambitious and charming twenty-something, eager to make his mark. Now he was in his sixties and what you can get away with in your twenties doesn't necessarily work several decades on. He himself was complaining about the lack of chemistry in the cast and the feeling was reciprocated. There were mutterings among cast members about his neediness and constant attempts to be the centre of attention. Again, it had worked with Mork; Simon was not the same.

He also upset a lot of people by bringing his rescue pug, Leonard, to the set. 'He brought it everywhere with him,' the source revealed. 'When he wasn't filming a scene, he was holding and petting and fawning over the dog.' Some people found it disruptive; Robin's attention seemed to be elsewhere

In all, the show was turning into a very unhappy experience and this was mirrored in the viewing figures. It started off with 15.52 million viewers – the highest-viewed premiere that autumn – but fell to just 5.23 million by the series finale. Williams was nominated for various awards for his role but didn't win anything. However, Sarah Michelle Gellar picked up the People's Choice Award for Favorite Actress in a New TV Series, which may have been somewhat galling.

In May 2014 it was announced that the show had been cancelled. So that had been his TV comeback. Not exactly the glorious return everyone had hoped for. And for a man who was already finding it hard to cope, it was a devastating blow.

In July of that year he was back in rehab. Publicly, it was denied that he'd had another relapse: 'After working back-to-back projects, Robin is simply taking the opportunity to fine-tune and focus on his continued commitment, of which he remains extremely proud,' said a statement. But it was clear to those around him that something was very, very wrong. He had been fretting for years about his film career, his television comeback hadn't worked out and, according to some, he was finding it really difficult to stay on the wagon.

Having spent a lifetime fighting them off, he was now overwhelmed by his demons. And when people get to that stage they no longer realise they have the support of a family behind them. As his daughter was to comment, Robin simply didn't realise how much he was loved.

'Reality is just a crutch for people who can't cope with drugs.'
ROBIN WILLIAMS

CHAPTER FIFTEEN

EPILOGUE: A COMEDIC GENIUS

'You'll have bad times but it'll always wake you up to the good stuff you weren't paying attention to.'

ROBIN WILLIAMS

No one can tell what finally pushes a person over the edge. Robin Williams had plunged into a terrible abyss but, while career setbacks undoubtedly played a part, he had been fighting depression all his life. Health and money concerns didn't help but what happened to him was the result of a lifelong struggle, not a series of setbacks that left him feeling down. And as his daughter Zelda pointed out after his death, he didn't realise how much he was loved. Even those who had professed to dislike him in his heyday were grief-stricken when they learned of his fate.

But Williams changed the face of light entertainment. He might have made a few ropy films but he made some excellent ones too, which have become a part of our popular culture. Even *Mork & Mindy*, a lightweight television show, is fondly mentioned by a generation. And he was the outstanding stand-up act of his era, an artist no one could take on with any hope of competing and someone who could reduce vast theatre audiences to helpless, weeping laughter. But to have the energy to do that would always betoken a darker side. And in a way, his attempt to control his wilder side could almost be seen as having a diminishing effect upon himself.

'It's been a sequence,' he told *Rolling Stone* as far back as 1991. 'With *Good Morning, Vietnam*, people said, "Ah, at last he's found a way to be funny and still be a little restrained." With *Dead Poets Society*, they went, "Oh, this is interesting – he's even more restrained." And with *Awakenings*, it'll be, "Look! He's medicated! He's gone even further. What's he playing next? He's playing a door." And after that? A black hole.'

Without wishing to become too much the amateur psychologist, that black hole was what he finally fell into, like a number of other outstanding comedians who were finally floored by a world with which they could not cope. Robin was often accused of being too sentimental: possibly, but too sensitive would probably be closer to the mark.

'Williams seemed to have an uncanny ability and vulnerability to take on so many personas,' Dwight

EPILOGUE: A COMEDIC GENIUS

DeWerth-Pallmeyer, associate professor of communication studies at Widener University in Chester, Pennsylvania, told the *Christian Science Monitor*. 'Williams could intellectually get inside characters in a nuanced way that reflected both the depth of the characters he played and his own intelligence.'

But to do that, of course, made him even more vulnerable: if he was portraying a damaged character, he had to feel that damage himself. And he was damaged, badly. He never stopped portraying the man-child because he never stopped *being* the man-child. Even his decidedly adult activities, drugs and the odd period of promiscuity arose from an inner neediness. Admittedly, he went through various debauched periods in his life but he himself was not actually a debauched man.

'There was also a depth of humanity in his work, an understanding of what it means to be different, and how everyone has a creative and generous side – he thoroughly understood and explored the impulse to connect with others at a very basic level, something that the best entertainers know how to tap in to in order to speak about larger truths,' Derek A. Burrill, associate professor of Media and Cultural Studies at UC Riverside in California told the *Christian Science Monitor*, comparing Williams to Tom Hanks, Bill Cosby, Peter Sellers and Richard Pryor – 'that special something'.

Williams also changed the look of stand-up, becoming a hugely important character in San Francisco's growing comedy scene and debuting a free-flying improvisational style that had not really been done before. He influenced a whole generation of up-and-coming comedians, not least Jim Carrey, who in his early days would do an impression of Mork. And he really raised the bar when it came to comedy: few could match his levels of energy and sense of anarchy. His legacy unquestionably remains.

And all that agonising about his career was not strictly necessary – he was actually one of the most successful actors of his generation. His movies have grossed a combined $3.2 billion in the United States and $5.2 billion worldwide, according to Box Office Mojo. He's been in thirteen films that have grossed more than $100 million in the US – pretty good going by anybody's standards. And he would have received even more off the back of DVD sales and rentals. The major plum roles might have been drying up but he lasted for thirty years at the top, far longer than all but a handful of actors. Many younger comedians who managed a few years as the hottest thing in town have now been largely forgotten but Robin Williams certainly hasn't, as was obvious from the reaction when he died.

Williams' ongoing status as a Hollywood player with clout was confirmed by the fact that, at the time of his death, 11 August 2014, he still had three films to be released. Those were *A Merry Friggin' Christmas*, about an estranged father and son taking a road trip together; *Night At The Museum: Secret Of The Tomb*, in which he reprised his role as Theodore Roosevelt in the second sequel in the popular franchise; and *Absolutely Anything*, a sci-fi tale starring Simon Pegg and

Kate Beckinsale, in which he voices an animated dog called Dennis. There was also *Boulevard*, another art-house movie which, at the time of writing, has no release date.

The endless talks about a sequel to *Mrs. Doubtfire* had also resumed, though, in the wake of his death, it seems unlikely to go ahead. Director Chris Columbus gave a statement to *Variety* after Robin died: 'His performances were unlike anything any of us had ever seen; they came from some spiritual and otherworldly place. He truly was one of the few people who deserved the title of "genius,"' he said.

Given that line-up, it does seem as though his financial difficulties were all in the mind. Perhaps it was ageing that got to him. He was in his sixties – no age at all these days – but Hollywood is always on the lookout for the new and Robin couldn't be said to be that anymore. But he was a true original, an enormously talented man who was able to move from stand-up to serious, as well as a kind-hearted and generous individual.

The legendary Robin Williams himself may no longer be with us but his star will continue to shine for many years to come.

> *'But only in their dreams can men be truly free.*
> *It was ever thus and always thus will be.'*
> JOHN KEATING (ROBIN WILLIAMS),
> *DEAD POETS SOCIETY* (1989)

TWENTY GREAT ROBIN WILLIAMS' JOKES

No book about Robin Williams would be complete without the jokes. Here are some of the best.

1. God gave men both a penis and a brain but, unfortunately, not enough blood supply to run both at the same time.

2. If it's the Psychic Network, why do they need a phone number?

3. Who the fuck came up with the idea of polygamy?! Who was having a marriage going, 'My one marriage isn't going too well, I'd like to double down.'?

4. The Chinese make everything! Even the 'Free Tibet' stickers.

5. Do you think God gets stoned? I think so… Look at the platypus.

6. Never pick a fight with an ugly person, they've got nothing to lose.

7. Politics: 'Poli' a Latin word meaning 'many' and 'tics' meaning 'bloodsucking creatures'.

8. And Honda has a car now that'll park itself. I'm like, 'Where were you when I was drinking?!'

9. I wonder what chairs think about all day: 'Oh, here comes another asshole.'

10. I want to thank my father… the man who, when I said I wanted to be an actor, he said,: 'Wonderful, just have a backup profession like welding.' Thank you.

11. Being a functioning alcoholic is kind of like being a paraplegic lap dancer – you can do it, just not as well as the others, really.

12. On the Immaculate Conception: The night that Mary said to Joe, 'Joe, I'm pregnant,' and Joe went, 'Holy Mother of God!' And she went, 'You're right! Aw, Jesus Christ, what a great name, Joe! That is so much better than Schmul! Way to go! I love you, Joe!'

13. People say satire is dead. It's not dead; it's alive and living in the White House.

14. We had gay burglars the other night; they broke in and rearranged the furniture.

15. You could talk about same-sex marriage but people who have been married [say] 'It's the same sex all the time.'

16. If women ran the world, we wouldn't have wars, just intense negotiations every twenty-eight days.

17. I walked into my son's room the other day and he's got four screens going at the same time. He's watching a movie on one screen, playing a game on another, downloading something on this one, texting on that one… People say, 'He's got ADHD.' Fuck that, he's multitasking!

18. 'I guess I should talk for a moment about the very serious subject of schizophrenia…' 'No, he doesn't!' 'Shut up, let him talk!'

19. If on your tax form it says, '$50,000 for snacks', MAYDAY! You've got yourself a cocaine problem.

20. Giving people tax rebates and then saying the economy is sound because they might spend it is like saying fat people are healthy because they might exercise.